Adobe
Illustrator™

CLASSROOM IN A BOOK

Library of Congress Catalog No.: 93-73014

ISBN: I-56830-052-2

10 9 8 7 6 5 4 3 2   First Printing: March 1994

The information in this book is furnished for informational use only, is subject to change without notice, and should not be construed as a commitment by Adobe Systems Incorporated. Adobe Systems Incorporated assumes no responsibility for any errors or inaccuracies that may appear in this book. The software and typefaces mentioned in this book are furnished under license and may be used or copied only in accordance with the terms of such license.

PANTONE®* Computer Video simulations used in this product may not match PANTONE-identified solid color standards. Use current PANTONE Color Reference Manuals for accurate color. *Pantone, Inc.'s check-standard trademark for color. PANTONE Color Computer Graphics" © Pantone, Inc. 1986, 1993.

Pantone, Inc. is the copyright owner of PANTONE Color Computer Graphics and Software, which are licensed to Adobe to distribute for use only in combination with Adobe Illustrator. PANTONE Color Computer Graphics and Software shall not be copied onto another diskette or into memory unless as part of the execution of Adobe Illustrator.

PostScript™ is a trademark of Adobe Systems Incorporated ("Adobe"), registered in the United States and elsewhere. PostScript can refer both to the PostScript language as specified by Adobe and to Adobe's implementation of its PostScript language interpreter.

The terms "PostScript printers," "PostScript files," or "PostScript drivers" refer, respectively, to printers, files, and driver programs written in or supporting the PostScript language. References in this book to the "PostScript language" are intended to emphasize Adobe's standard definition of that language.

Adobe, the Adobe logo, the Adobe Press logo, Acrobat, Adobe Dimensions, Adobe Garamond, Adobe Illustrator, Adobe Photoshop, Adobe Premiere, Adobe Type Manager, Adobe Separator, Adobe Streamline, Adobe Teach, ATM, Classroom in a Book, Classroom in a Box, Distiller, Madrone, Minion, and PostScript are trademarks of Adobe Systems Incorporated, which may be registered in certain jurisdictions. Barmeno, Bellvue is a trademark and Berthold City is a registered trademark of H. Berthold AG. Fruitiger, Helvetica, and Times are trademarks of Linotype-Hell AG and/or its subsidiaries. Gill Sans is a trademark of The Monotype Corporation, registered in the US Patent and Trademark Office and elsewhere. Agfa is a registered trademark of Agfa division, Miles, Inc. Apple, Macintosh, and LaserWriter are registered trademarks, and Quadra, QuickDraw, QuickTime, System 6, System 7, and TrueType are trademarks of Apple Computer, Inc. MacroMind Director is a trademark of Macromedia, Inc. CameraMan and Movie Play are registered tradmarks of Vision Software. All other brand and product names are trademarks or registered trademarks of their respective holders. Photograph liscensed from THE BETTMAN ARCHIVE.

Printed in the United States of America by Shepard Poorman Communications, Indianapolis, Indiana.

Published simultaneously in Canada.

Adobe Press books are published and distributed by Hayden Books, a division of Prentice Hall Computer Publishing. For individual orders, or for educational, corporate, or retail sales accounts, call 1-800-428-5331. For information, address Hayden Books, 201 W. 103rd Street, Indianapolis IN 46290.

CONTENTS

INTRODUCTION

The Adobe Illustrator™ program is one of the most popular illustration software programs sold today. The Adobe Illustrator *Classroom in a Book*™ is a set of lessons designed to teach you how to use Adobe Illustrator.

Created by the Educational Services group at Adobe Systems, Inc., *Classroom in a Book* is a project-based series of lessons that you can complete at your own pace. You can expect to spend between 20 and 30 hours with this product.

HOW DOES IT WORK?

Classroom in a Book consists of a series of design projects with complete information for creating them. Once you've learned some Pen tool basics, you'll spend time creating projects. Within this context, you'll work on a poster design, postcard, stamp design, book cover, and packaging—all of the kinds of tasks you might do when working with this drawing program.

Working in the context of actual projects, you'll learn different techniques for putting together your knowledge of many different Adobe Illustrator techniques.

WHO SHOULD USE IT?

Classroom in a Book is designed for users at many levels. If you're new to Adobe Illustrator, you'll get a good grounding in all the basic features. If you have been using Adobe Illustrator for a while, you'll find *Classroom in a Book* teaches many advanced features that are included with the latest version of Adobe Illustrator.

This book is meant to be used in conjunction with the documentation provided with Adobe Illustrator. You'll still need to refer to the *Adobe Illustrator User Guide*, *Tutorial*, and *Beyond the Basics*.

SELF-PACED LEARNING

Using *Classroom in a Book* is similar to taking a 30-hour training course. In this case, you get to choose when and where you do the work. Final exam scheduling is also up to you.

When you have completed the projects in this book, you'll know all the basic features and most of the features of the Adobe Illustrator program.

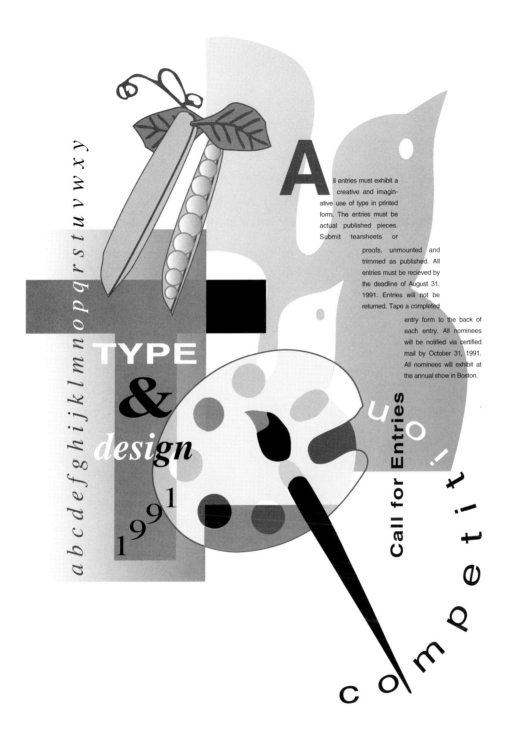

a b c d e f g h i j k l m n o p q r s t u v w x y

TYPE

&

design

1991

A

ll entries must exhibit a
creative and imagin-
ative use of type in printed
form. The entries must be
actual published pieces.
Submit tearsheets or
proofs, unmounted and
trimmed as published. All
entries must be recieved by
the deadline of August 31,
1991. Entries will not be
returned. Tape a completed
entry form to the back of
each entry. All nominees
will be notified via certified
mail by October 31, 1991.
All nominees will exhibit at
the annual show in Boston.

Call for Entries

competition

GETTING STARTED

Before you begin using Adobe Illustrator *Classroom in a Book*, you need to make sure that your system is set up correctly and that you have installed all the necessary software.

Although we can't include an Adobe Illustrator *Instructor in a Book*, we will provide all the help we can to get your system set up and ready to go.

WHAT YOU NEED TO DO

To get ready to use *Classroom in a Book*, you need to do the following things. (We'll give you more details later.)

• Check the system requirements.

• Install Adobe Illustrator and Adobe Type Manager, as described in the *Getting Started* booklet that came with Adobe Illustrator.

• Install the fonts that we have included with the *Classroom in a Book*. (If you have already installed the fonts that came with Adobe Illustrator 4.0, you can skip this part. Copy the *Classroom in a Book* files that come with this package to your hard drive.

CHECKING THE SYSTEM REQUIREMENTS

The system requirements are the same as those for the Adobe Illustrator 4.0 program, except that you need a CD-ROM drive. If you are already running Adobe Illustrator 4.0, skip down to the section named "Special considerations."

System requirements

More specifically, the Adobe Illustrator 4.0 system requirements are

• An IBM®PC, AT®, PS/2™, or a 100 percent compatible computer using a 386™, 386sx, or 486 processor

• 4MB of random-access memory (RAM)

• Hard drive with at least 12 megabytes (MB) of free disk space

• Microsoft MS-DOS 3.13 or greater with Windows 3.0 environment or greater

• VGA, Super VGA, 16-bit or 24-bit display adapter supported by Windows 3.0 or greater

• VGA resolution display set at 640×480 in Windows setup

• Any PostScript™ printer or other PC/Windows compatible graphic output device.

Special considerations

In addition to the general requirements, there are several more that apply only to *Classroom in a Book*.

• To use the *Classroom in a Book* files, you need a CD-ROM drive.

• To take advantage of the lessons in this book, you need a color monitor.

INSTALLING THE SOFTWARE

You need to install the Adobe Illustrator program with Adobe Type Manager™, the special *Classroom in a Book* student fonts, and the *Classroom in a Book* files.

Installing Adobe Illustrator and the Adobe Type Manager program

Install the Adobe Illustrator and Adobe Type Manager programs. Adobe Illustrator *Classroom in a Book* does not include the Adobe Illustrator program software. You must purchase the software separately. The *Getting Started* guide that comes with Adobe Illustrator 4.0 includes complete instructions for installing both Adobe Illustrator and the Adobe Type Manager (ATM™) program.

Installing the fonts

The *Classroom in a Book* electronic files use several special Adobe™ Type 1 fonts. These fonts (both outline and bitmapped) are included in the Adobe Illustrator program software. You must install these fonts in your system before you can use the electronic files. The fonts needed for this book include the following:

Adobe Garamond™
Gill Sans®
Helvetica
Poplar™
Times

Complete instructions for installing Adobe Type 1 fonts are included in the *Getting Started* guide that comes with Adobe Illustrator 4.0. See the section named "Using the ATM Program," and the subsection named "Using Adobe Type 1 fonts."

Copying the *Classroom in a Book* files

The *Classroom in a Book* CD-ROM disk includes directories containing all the electronic files for the *Classroom in a Book* lessons. These directories are included:

AI4CIB
    Disk 1
    Disk 2

To copy all of these files, drag the Adobe Illustrator AI4CIB directory icon onto your hard disk drive. This directory includes the two lesson file directories.

If you have limited hard disk space, you may want to copy only the files for one or two lessons at a time.

Creating a Project folder

While you're working through *Classroom in a Book*, you will create and save many Adobe Illustrator files.

We recommend that you make a Project folder and put your work files there.

GETTING READY TO ROLL

Now that you've got everything installed, there are a few more things you need to know before you begin.

You should know Windows™ basics before you use *Classroom in a Book*. If you can use a menu, resize a window, and open and save files, you know enough to use this book.

Several of the lessons will teach you tasks in Adobe Illustrator. After several skills have been introduced, review projects are included to practice the techniques learned up to that point. After the first three review projects, more lessons will teach other new skills followed by more review projects.

Using the final files

A completed file for each project in this book is included in the Instruct directory. The files are as follows:

DOVPOFIN.AI (lesson 4)
POSTFIN.AI (lesson 5)
STAMPFIN.AI (lesson 6)
MASKFIN.AI (lesson 11)
BAYFIN.AI (lesson 12)
SEEDFIN.AI (lesson 13)

You can take a look at the final file before you begin a project. We recommend that you resize the final file and leave it open in case you want to refer to it while you are working on a project.

The final files for the lessons are locked. You will not be able to save any changes to the final files.

Moving on

Now that your system is set up and ready to go, it's time to begin learning Adobe Illustrator. Lesson 1 begins with a quick overview of the Adobe Illustrator program's tools.

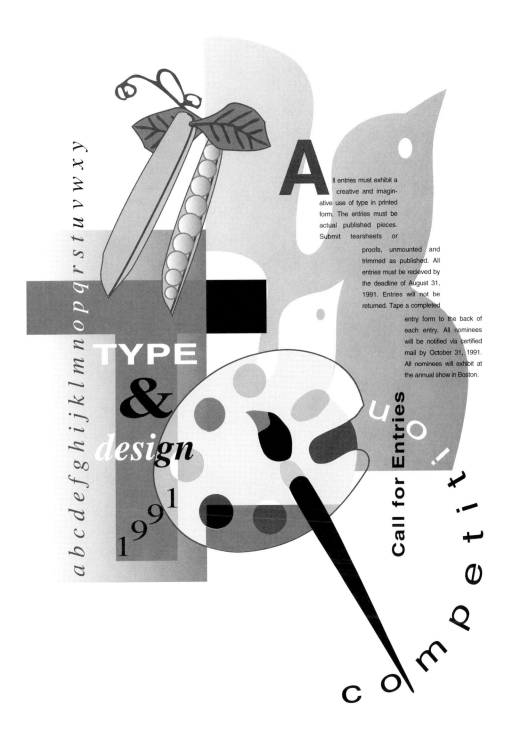

abcdefghijklmnopqrstuvwxy

TYPE

&

design

1991

All entries must exhibit a creative and imaginative use of type in printed form. The entries must be actual published pieces. Submit tearsheets or proofs, unmounted and trimmed as published. All entries must be recieved by the deadline of August 31, 1991. Entries will not be returned. Tape a completed entry form to the back of each entry. All nominees will be notified via certified mail by October 31, 1991. All nominees will exhibit at the annual show in Boston.

Call for Entries

competition

Lesson

1

Lesson 1: Using the Drawing Tools

The Adobe Illustrator application program is a drawing program that combines the speed of a computer with the control of fine detail formerly possible only when drawing by hand. The *Classroom in a Book* for Adobe Illustrator will guide you through thirteen creative lessons that will assist you in mastering your skills in using Adobe Illustrator as a powerful drawing tool.

STARTING AT THE BEGINNING

You will begin lesson one by learning important Adobe Illustrator terminology and tools. Also, you will learn to use the Pen tool that is so popular to the Adobe Illustrator application.

After adjust the preferences dialog box, you will open a file that includes a template. A template is a black and white bitmapped image that can be traced to create artwork in the Adobe Illustrastor program. You will use the template as a tracing guide in this lesson.

Note: The Num Lock key on the keyboard must be activated if the student plans to use the number pad for the lessons to come.

To start the application

1 Start the DOS computer, and locate the Adobe Illustrator program.

2 Launch the Adobe Illustrator™ program by double-clicking its icon.

Before you begin using the program, you will set the Preferences back to their default values.

3 Choose Preferences from the Edit menu. The Preferences dialog box will appear on your screen.

4 Compare the values on your screen to the ones in the illustration below. Make sure that the values are the same.

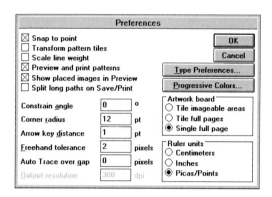

5 Click the Type Preferences button. Make sure that the values in the Type Preferences dialog box match those in the illustration below.

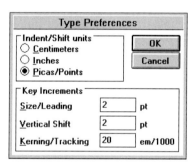

6 Click OK to close the Type Preferences dialog box.

To open a file

1 Click OK to close the Preferences dialog box.

2 Choose Place template from the File menu.

3 Under Format choose TIFF (.TIF).

4 Double-click the *ILLCIB* subdirectory under Directories.

5 Click the file called *STUDTMP.TIF* under Files, and click the Place button.

THE PAGE

Looking at the template, you'll notice that it is not entirely visible on the screen.

1 Choose Fit Artwork In Window from the View menu to see the whole page.

Your screen should now look like this:

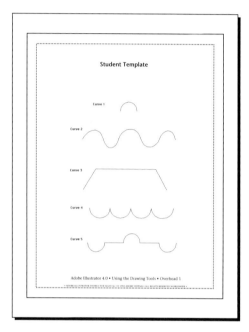

What you see now is the Adobe Illustrator program's drawing area, or artwork board. The two rectangles show the page boundary and the imageable area. The outside rectangle defines the page boundary. The inside dotted rectangle defines the imageable area, the area where your printer can print.

These areas change depending on the settings you choose in the Preferences dialog box and the Page Layout dialog box, and on the type of printer you are using.

2 Choose Actual Size from the View menu to return the template to its actual dimensions and size on the screen.

USING THE TOOLBOX

The first time you open a document, the toolbox appears on the left side of the screen. The toolbox can be modified to meet your needs; several of these options are covered below.

The tools

There are 40 tools in the toolbox, and 16 tools are seen at a given time.

The toolbox

The default toolbox consists of the tools you see when you first open the program. To use a tool in the toolbox, you move the pointer to one of the tools, click the mouse button, and move the pointer back to the window.

Each tool has an associated pointer. For example, the Selection tool has an arrow pointer; the Zoom-in tool, a magnifying pointer; and the Type tool, an I-beam. The Status Line in the bottom of the window shows which tool is selected.

Pop-up tools

Other tools in the toolbox are "hidden" behind the tools you see. You access these tools by positioning the pointer on the arrow to the right of a tool, holding down the mouse button, and dragging to the right.

To select one of these tools, drag to the right and release the mouse button over the tool of your choice.

Notice that the selected tool moves into the toolbox after you choose the tool.

Throughout this class we will use the Reset Toolbox command in the View menu. This command returns the default toolbox.

At any time, you can reset the toolbox to its default by choosing Reset Toolbox from the Toolbox Options submenu under the View menu.

The tools

The following figure shows all the tools in the toolbox.

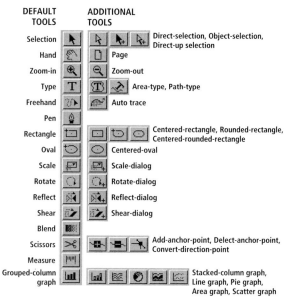

Showing and hiding the toolbox

If you want more room to work, you can hide the toolbox. The Show Toolbox command under the View menu controls whether the toolbox is visible or invisible. If the Show Toolbox command is checked, the toolbox is visible; if the Show Toolbox command is not checked, the toolbox is hidden.

Using large or small tools

You can specify whether the toolbox displays large or small tool icons by choosing Large Tools or Small Tools from the Toolbox Options submenu under the View menu. If you cannot view all of the large tools on your monitor, choose Small Tools.

Using a floating toolbox

If you choose the Floating command from the Toolbox Options submenu under the View menu, you can change the size and shape of the toolbox to suit your needs. To change the shape of the floating toolbox, position the pointer on any corner of the toolbox and drag to define the new shape.

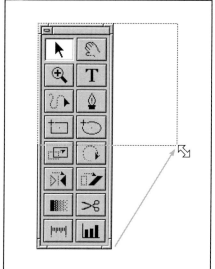

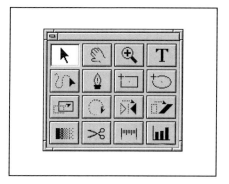

When you change the display of the floating toolbox, the additional tools will display either above, below, to the right, or to the left of the selected tool in the toolbox, depending on the tool's current location in the toolbox.

Using the Status Line

The Adobe Illustrator workspace contains a Status Line at the bottom of the screen. The Status Line is divided into seven sections.

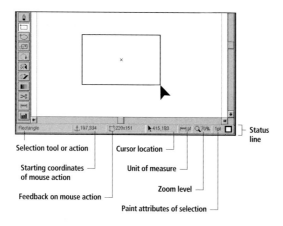

Selection tool or action

Starting coordinates
of mouse action

Feedback on mouse action

Cursor location

Unit of measure

Zoom level

Paint attributes of selection

Status line

• The first section of the Status Line displays the name of the selected tool or, in some cases, the action you will perform with the currently selected tool. For example, when you select the hand tool, the Status Line reads "Scroll."

The text in the Status Line also changes to reflect actions you are performing. For example, if you are copying an object in an artwork document by dragging the object while holding down the Alt key, the Status Line reads "Copy." If you hold down the Shift key while moving an object, the Status Line reads "Constrain."

The text may also display miscellaneous information such as the PostScript filename, or the font name and size.

• The second part of the Status Line displays the *x* and *y* coordinates of an object from the beginning of the mouse action of a transformation; if no action is occurring, the line is blank.

• The third section of the Status Line gives feedback on a transformation, such as the location of an object's centerpoint, an object's size, or the degree of rotation; if no action is occurring, the line is blank.

• The fourth section of the Status Line displays the *x* and *y* coordinates of the cursor's location on-screen.

• The fifth section of the Status Line shows the unit of measure that is currently selected in the Preferences dialog box (centimeters, inches, or picas/points).

• The sixth section of the Status Line displays the current magnification level of your artwork.

• The last section of the Status Line displays the stroke and fill attribute of the currently selected object.

Selection tools

There are four selection tools: the Selection tool, the Direct-selection tool, the Object-selection tool, and the Direct-up selection tool.

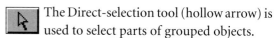 The Selection tool (solid arrow) operates just like the standard selection pointer. It can be used to select points, lines, and curves for moving or editing.

The Direct-selection tool (hollow arrow) is used to select parts of grouped objects.

The Object-selection tool (solid arrow with a +) is used to select all the parts of an entire path or all parts of grouped objects.

The Direct-up selection tool (hollow arrow with a +) is used to add to grouped selections. Each successive click adds another layer of grouped objects to the selection.

Window management tools

The Hand tool allows you to move the page around on the screen and to view areas that are off the edges of the page.

1 Click the Hand tool in the toolbox.

2 Hold down the mouse button and drag the page and artwork around on the desktop.

3 Move the page so that curve 1 is in the middle of the screen.

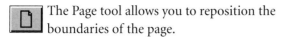 The Page tool allows you to reposition the boundaries of the page.

The zoom tools are used to enlarge or reduce your view of specific areas of an image, which is similar to enlarging or reducing on a copy machine. Zoom in to achieve more precise drawing and editing. The Zoom-in tool (magnifying glass with a plus sign) increases magnification (or zooms in) up to four times. The Zoom-out tool (magnifying glass with a minus sign) reduces magnification. Either of the zoom tools allows you to hold down the mouse and drag a marquee rectangle to zoom in or out at that exact area.

Clicks	⊕	⊖
+4	1600%	
+3	800%	
+2	400%	
+1	200%	
0	100%	100%
-1		50%
-2		25%
-3		12.5%
-4		6.25%

4 Select the Zoom-in tool and click the mouse over curve 1 to enlarge your view of the curve. Continue to click until you cannot zoom in anymore.

5 Select the Zoom-out tool.

6 Click the mouse button several times to reduce your view.

7 Choose Actual Size from the View menu to return to actual size.

Type tools

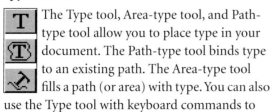 The Type tool, Area-type tool, and Path-type tool allow you to place type in your document. The Path-type tool binds type to an existing path. The Area-type tool fills a path (or area) with type. You can also use the Type tool with keyboard commands to create all three kinds of type.

Drawing tools

The Freehand, Auto Trace, Pen, Rectangle, and Oval tools are all drawing tools.

The Freehand tool is used to create a line that would be too complex or time-consuming to accomplish with the Pen tool. The Freehand tool is used "like a pencil." You drag the mouse and a line appears on the screen.

The Auto Trace tool is used to trace over templates automatically. A detailed template that would take hours to trace with the Pen or Freehand tool might be traced with the Auto Trace tool in a minute.

The Pen tool is the real workhorse of the Adobe Illustrator program. Using this tool, you can draw a multitude of different lines, curves, and combinations without having to stop and change to another drawing tool. The Pen tool can be used to trace over templates, just as you might use a pencil and tracing paper to trace lines from a photograph. The Pen tool is best used to create sweeping, smooth curves and clean, straight lines with a low-to-medium level of detail. Notice what happens in the Status Line when you click the Pen tool. You see which tool you have selected. For some tools, you are also prompted about what to do next.

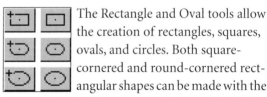 The Rectangle and Oval tools allow the creation of rectangles, squares, ovals, and circles. Both square-cornered and round-cornered rectangular shapes can be made with the Rectangle tools. The program also provides dialog boxes for these tools, so you can specify exact sizes for these shapes.

Transformation tools

 The Scale, Rotate, Reflect, and Shear tools are the "power tools" of the Adobe Illustrator program. An object or part of an object can be enlarged, reduced in size, rotated, mirrored, or slanted with these tools.

The Blend tool creates a series of transformations between two objects. You can transform one shape into another, a color into another, or a line weight into another. The Blend tool is indispensable for gradual shading of objects.

Anchor point tools

 These tools let you split paths, add or delete anchor points, or convert direction points.

Miscellaneous tools

Like a ruler on a real drawing board, the Measure tool not only measures horizontal and vertical distance, but also provides you with the distance "as the crow flies," as well as the exact angle in degrees between two specified points on the page.

Graph tools

The graph tools let you automatically create graphs from numbers. If you hold down the pointer on the button next to the Grouped-column graph tool, you can see the six different kinds of graphs that are available in the program.

CONCEPTS OF ADOBE ILLUSTRATOR

Before you begin using the Adobe Illustrator program, it's helpful to understand a fundamental difference between the drawing model used by Adobe Illustrator and the drawing model used by other electronic illustration programs, such as Icon.

When you use tools such as Icon, the mouse acts very much like a pen. You drag the mouse and a line appears on the screen. With the Adobe Illustrator program, you can create lines and curves in several ways, and you can then perform powerful editing functions to perfect the drawn lines.

One method of drawing is to build lines and curves by specifying points with the Pen tool. The Adobe Illustrator program then connects the points. The process is similar to what children do when they create pictures by connecting dots. With the Adobe Illustrator program, the technique comes in knowing where to place the dots to create the desired lines and curves.

A second method of drawing is to use the Freehand tool to trace over a template or draw freehand lines or curves. Adobe Illustrator will then take the sketch line you've drawn and convert it to a series of points and lines that can be edited.

A third way of creating paths is to let the Auto Trace tool do it for you. Any template with good contrast and solid areas can be successfully auto traced with this method. You can even auto trace only a portion of a template, if you wish.

Whenever you create curves or lines with one of these methods, the resulting points and lines have two common features: anchor points and direction points.

Each curve in the Adobe Illustrator program is defined by four points: two anchor points and two direction lines. Anchor points determine where a curve starts and ends. Direction lines determine the shape of the curve. A curve or line defined by two anchor points and two direction lines is called a segment.

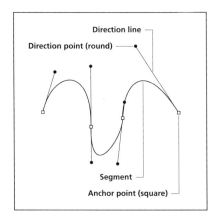

The Adobe Illustrator program is very different from any drawing product you have ever seen. It allows you to create artwork that is saved as pure PostScript™ language code, which means tremendous advantages in clarity of output, ease of editing, and portability to other desktop publishing software and hardware.

The most common method of using Adobe Illustrator (but not the only method) is to trace over a scanned image of uncopyrighted art or a pencil drawing. The following session will concentrate on the tools used in Adobe Illustrator to trace images.

DRAWING A SINGLE CURVE

You will begin by using the pen tool to trace *curve 1* on the page.

Drawing Curve 1

1 Choose Toolbox Options from the View menu and Reset Toolbox from the submenu.

2 Make sure that curve 1 is visible on your screen and that you are working at Actual Size.

3 Select the Pen tool. (You'll see the x pointer when you position the Pen tool on the page; this indicates that you are beginning a new path.)

4 Place the x at the left end of the first curve on the template.

5 Hold down the mouse button and drag the pointer up (in the direction that you want the curve to go), and then release the mouse button. When you release the mouse button, the pointer changes to a +; this tells you that you are now continuing a path rather than starting a new one.

You have just created an anchor point and a direction point. The anchor point determines where the curve begins and ends, while the direction point determines how much it curves and in which direction.

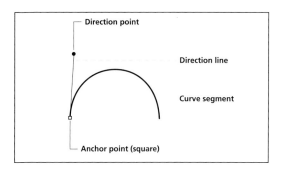

6 Move the + pointer to the other end of the curve.

7 Hold down the mouse button, and drag the direction point down to fit the curve to the template; then release the mouse button.

8 To correct a mistake, press the Backspace key twice, and try steps 4–7 again.

9 Move the pointer to the toolbox, and click the Pen tool to end the path.

A RULE OF THUMB FOR TRACING CURVES

There are a few tips to remember in drawing curves, the first one is the One-Third rule.

The One-Third rule

The One-Third rule suggests that as you draw a curved line and drag the direction point toward the direction of the curve, you make the distance between the first anchor point and the first direction point about one-third of the length of the curve segment you are tracing. It helps to imagine how long the curve you are tracing would be if it were a straight line.

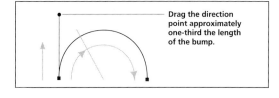

Editing direction points

You can edit a path in several ways: by its anchor points, direction points, or even its curves.

1 Use the Selection tool (solid arrow) to select the curve segment. Notice that both endpoints (anchor points) of the curve appear as small, hollow squares. Also notice that a direction line and direction point are visible from the anchor point on either side of the selected curve segment.

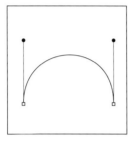

2 Click away from the artwork to deselect everything.

3 Click the curve.

4 Use the Selection tool to drag a direction point (at the end of the direction line) in any direction to change the overall shape of the curve. Select an anchor point in order to see the direction lines and points attached to that anchor point.

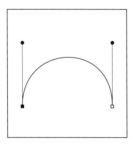
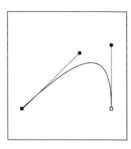

Editing anchor points

1 Use the Selection tool (solid arrow) to select the rightmost anchor point.

2 Use the Selection tool to move the anchor point up and down, left and right.

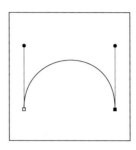
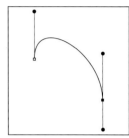

Editing curve segments

With this technique, you can edit two direction points at once.

1 Click away from the artwork to deselect everything.

2 Use the Selection tool (solid arrow) to select the curve itself, but not the anchor points.

3 Move the top of the curve up and down. Notice that you can't move the curve left or right across an anchor point.

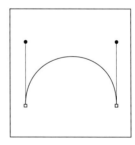
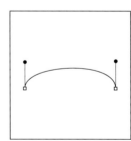

Moving a whole path

1 Choose the Object-selection tool (solid arrow with a +).

2 Click the curve. This selects the whole path.

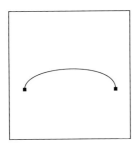
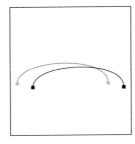

3 Position the pointer on the path and drag it. Notice that its position on the page is changed. The Status Line changes to "Move" when you begin dragging.

Copying a path

1 Using the Object-selection tool, drag the curve as if you were moving it, and then hold down the Alternate key. The pointer changes to a double arrow (one solid, one hollow), and the Status Line changes to "Copy."

2 Release the mouse button, and then release the Alternate key. Be sure to release the mouse button *before* you release the Alternate key.

3 Press the Delete or Backspace key to erase the copy.

Transform Again command

1 Use the Object-selection tool to select the entire original curve.

2 Begin dragging the path, hold down the Alternate key, and drag a copy of the path to the right about half an inch. Release the mouse button, and then release the Alternate key.

3 Choose Transform Again several times from the Arrange menu. Transform Again repeats the last command, in this case move-and-copy.

4 Drag a selection marquee to select all the curves.

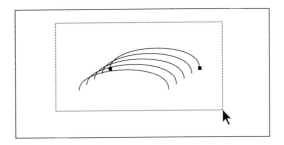

5 Press the Delete or Backspace key to clear the screen.

DRAWING MULTIPLE CURVES

You will now practice what you have learned about drawing a single curve to create multiple curves.

Drawing Curve 2

1 Select the Pen tool.

2 Place the x on the leftmost side of the curve, hold the mouse button down, and drag the direction point up. Release the mouse button.

3 Place the + pointer on the other side of the bump, hold the mouse button down, and drag the direction point down. Release the mouse button.

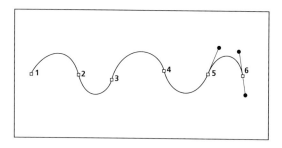

4 Continue placing and dragging up and down, and tracing the curve until you complete the curve.

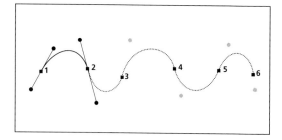

5 Click the Pen tool in the toolbox to end the path. Use the Selection tool if you want to move any curves or direction points.

6 Use the Object-selection tool to select the entire path.

7 Press the Delete or Backspace key to erase the path.

8 Draw the entire path again.

MORE RULES OF THUMB FOR TRACING CURVES

Below are two more helpful tips to remember when drawing curves.

The Bump rule

Whenever you draw a curve, you can use the Bump rule to determine where to place each anchor point. The Bump rule says to place the anchor points (1) on either side of each bump, rather than at the top of a bump, or (2) wherever a line changes its direction or tightness of curvature. Draw one bump at a time. This is the most efficient way to draw multiple curves within one path. You could draw multiple curves by creating more points, but, for the sake of efficiency and control, the Bump rule is very important.

Right. Place the anchor point wherever the curves change direction.

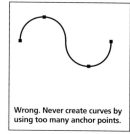

Wrong. Never create curves by using too many anchor points.

The Stride rule

Take big steps. Place anchor points as far apart as possible while still fitting the curve.

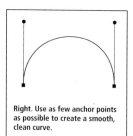

Right. Use as few anchor points as possible to create a smooth, clean curve.

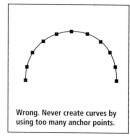

Wrong. Never create curves by using too many anchor points.

Removing and replacing a curve

1 Choose the Selection tool (solid arrow).

2 Click away from the artwork to deselect everything.

3 Click the top of the second bump on the curve to select the segment.

TIP: IF YOU WANT TO DRAW A PERFECTLY HORIZONTAL, VERTICAL, OR 45-DEGREE LINE, HOLD DOWN THE SHIFT KEY WHEN YOU PLACE THE ANCHOR POINTS.

4 Press the Delete or Backspace key to remove the curve segment.

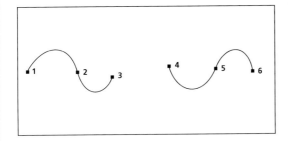

5 Select the Zoom-in tool, and click once to zoom in.

6 Select the Pen tool.

7 Position the pointer on the left anchor point bordering the dropped segment, hold down the mouse button, and drag up to create a direction line. This will continue that curve and give you control of the direction point for that anchor point.

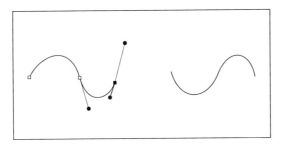

8 Position the pointer on the end of the other line. Hold down the mouse button and drag to fit the curve. As soon as you begin dragging the second point, you will have control of the direction points for that anchor point. Release the mouse button when you have finished.

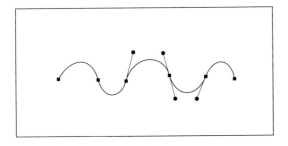

9 Click the Pen tool to end the path.

DRAWING STRAIGHT LINES

You can also create straight lines with the Pen tool. You draw straight lines by clicking and releasing the mouse instead of clicking and dragging the mouse as you did in drawing a curve.

Drawing Curve 3

1 Choose Actual Size from the View menu.

2 If necessary, scroll until you can see both curve 3 and curve 4 on the screen.

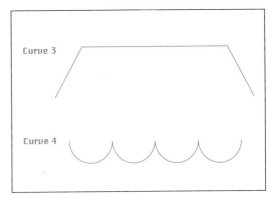

3 Select the Pen tool.

4 Position the pointer at the bottom left leg of curve 3, and click the mouse button. Do *not* drag.

5 Move the pointer up to the top of the segment, and click the mouse button again. You see a line between the two points where you clicked.

6 Hold down the Shift key, and click the corner on the right.

Holding down the Shift key when you click the third point creates a straight horizontal line. The Shift (or "constrain") key keeps lines at 90 degrees or 45 degrees, boxes square, and circles round.

7 Click the final corner of the shape.

DRAWING CURVED PATHS WITH CORNERS

By learning how to draw and create corners with the pen tool, you will increase the flexibility of your drawing.

Drawing Curve 4

1 Move the pointer to the beginning of curve 4.

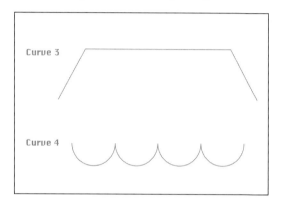

2 Place the pointer on the leftmost end of the curve, hold down the mouse button, and drag down in the direction of the curve.

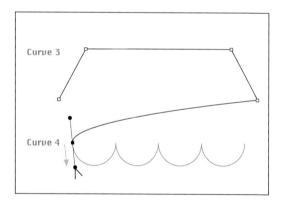

Notice that you have a line connecting the last point in curve 3 with the first point in curve 4. This is because you did not click the Pen tool to end the path of curve 3 before you moved on to curve 4.

Notice that the Status Line reads "Pen: click or drag next anchor" and the pointer is a +.

3 Choose Undo from the Edit menu.

4 Click the Pen tool.

Notice that the Status Line has changed to read "Pen: click or drag first anchor" and the pointer is an x.

5 Place the x pointer on the leftmost end of the curve, hold down the mouse button, and drag down in the direction of the curve.

6 Place the + on the other end of the first curve, and drag up as usual, completing the first curve.

7 Position the pointer on the last anchor point you drew, hold down the Alternate key, and drag the direction point down to change the direction of the next curve. Holding down the Alternate key allows you to turn a corner or change the direction of a curve.

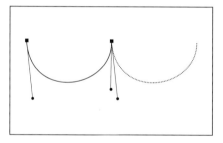

8 Finish drawing the next bump of the path, dragging up. Repeat the process for the rest of the shape.

9 Click the Pen tool to end the path.

10 Use the Object-selection tool to select the entire path and delete it. Then redraw the path.

DRAWING CURVES AND STRAIGHT LINES IN ONE PATH

The ability to draw curves and straight lines in one continuous path will allow you to draw almost any shape imaginable.

Drawing Curve 5

1 Scroll to reposition the page so that curve 5 is in the center of the screen.

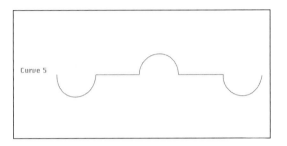

2 Select the Pen tool.

3 Position the x pointer on the leftmost end of the curve, and drag down, in the direction of the curve.

4 Place the + pointer on the other end of the leftmost curve, and drag up, completing the first curve.

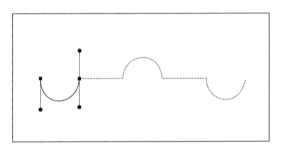

5 Position the + pointer on the last anchor point you drew, hold down the Alternate key, and click the mouse button.

6 Move the + pointer to the other end of the straight line segment, hold down the Shift key, and click the mouse button.

7 Position the + pointer on the last point you drew, hold down the Alternate key, and drag the direction point up to set the direction of the next curve.

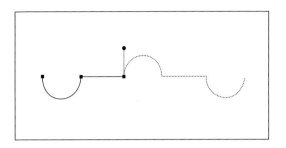

8 Finish drawing the next bump of the path, dragging down until the line conforms to the template.

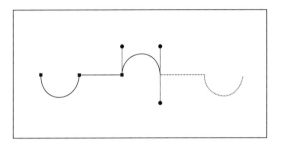

9 Draw the next straight line by clicking the last anchor point, holding down the Shift key, and clicking at the end of the line.

10 Position the + pointer on the end of the straight line.

11 Hold down the mouse button and the Alternate key, and drag the direction point to set the direction of the final curve.

12 Position the + pointer on the end of the template, hold down the mouse button, and drag to create the final curve.

13 Click the Pen tool to end the path.

TIP: YOU CAN RELEASE THE MOUSE BUTTON AT ANY TIME WHILE DRAWING WITH THE FREEHAND TOOL. TO CONTINUE DRAWING A CONTINUOUS PATH, PLACE THE FREEHAND TOOL POINTER ON THE LAST ANCHOR POINT, HOLD DOWN THE MOUSE BUTTON, AND CONTINUE TO DRAW.

USING KEYBOARD ALTERNATIVES

Many operations in the Adobe Illustrator program can be performed by holding down the Control key while you press another specific key or keys. You can use these keyboard alternatives to execute commands in menus as well as to access tools.

Alternatives for menu commands

When you open menus, you see a Control key alternative to the right of many of the commands. You can use these commands instead of choosing a command from a menu with the mouse.

Alternatives for accessing tools

You can access many tools from the keyboard.

1 Select the Pen tool in the toolbox, and move the pointer into the window. You see that the pointer changes to an x, and you see in the Status Line that you have selected the Pen tool.

2 Hold down the Control key. You see the pointer of the current selection tool (whichever selection tool is currently in the toolbox), and the Status Line changes accordingly. As long as you hold down the Control key, you have the selection pointer; when you release the Control key, the pointer returns to the Pen tool pointer.

Throughout this manual, you will see references to these keyboard alternatives in the sidebar to the left of the exercises.

Note: When using keyboard alternatives, you should always press the Control key first, and then press the other keys. The reason for this has to do with editing text. In text mode, if you press the Space bar, you won't get the Hand tool; instead, you will get a space in your text.

3 Release the Control key.

4 Hold down and then release the Space bar.

Common keyboard alternatives:

- Space bar: Hand tool
- Control key and Space bar: Zoom-in tool
- Control key, Space bar, and Alternate key: Zoom-out tool
- Control key: current selection tool

5 Release all the keys.

DRAWING WITH THE FREEHAND TOOL

Using the Freehand tool is similar to drawing with a pencil. The path on the screen follows the path you draw with the mouse.

1 Choose Close from the File menu. Do not save changes.

2 Choose New from the File menu.

3 Choose Place template, from the File menu. The Place Template dialog box appears. Choose TIFF for Format and select *FREETMP.TIF* and click Place.

4 Choose Toolbox Options from the View menu, and Reset Toolbox from the submenu.

5 Select the Zoom-in tool. Move the pointer to the middle of the leaf, and click once to zoom in. Select the Freehand tool (the tool below the Type tool in the toolbox).

6 Move the pointer to the edge of the leaf, and press and hold the mouse button. Trace along the outside edges of the leaf, holding the mouse button down while you draw. Trace all the way around the leaf until you are back where you started.

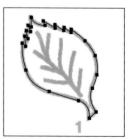

Note: If you make a mistake along the way, you can correct it with the eraser just before you release the mouse button.

Press the Control key, and the pointer will become hollow. This is the erase function of the Freehand tool. Hold the Control key and back up over the line to erase the mistake. Release the Control key after you have erased the mistake, and continue drawing the line. Do not release the mouse button.

7 When the pointer is over the point at which you started, release the mouse button to close the path.

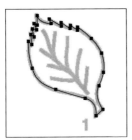 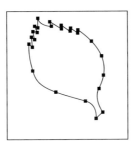

As soon as you release the mouse button, the Freehand tool will create a series of anchor points and direction points where you drew the line. These points are completely editable, just like points made with the Pen tool.

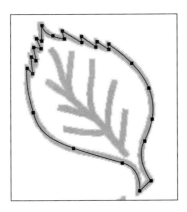

8 Choose Artwork Only from the View menu.

9 Choose Close from the File menu. Do not save changes.

DRAWING WITH THE AUTO TRACE TOOL

You can use the Auto Trace tool to automatically trace certain shapes on a template.

Tracing templates with the Auto Trace tool

1 Choose New from the File menu. Choose Place template from the File menu, choose TIFF for format, select *UMBTMP.TIF*, and click Place.

2 Choose Toolbox options from the View menu, and Reset toolbox from the submenu.

3 Select the Auto Trace tool.

4 Position the pointer on the outside edge of the template, and click the mouse button. Wait a few seconds for the Auto Trace tool to do its work.

You should now see the path that the Auto Trace tool has traced around the template. This path is made up of anchor points and direction points and is completely editable.

5 Choose Close from the File menu. Do not save changes.

Auto tracing only part of a template

The Auto Trace tool also lets you trace over part of a template.

1 Choose New from the File menu. Choose Place Template from the File menu, choose TIFF for format, select *PEATMP.TIF*, and click Place.

2 Select the Auto Trace tool.

3 Position the pointer on the edge of the pea pod, and click the mouse button to trace the entire shape.

4 Press the Delete or Backspace key twice to erase the path.

Note: The Bits Clockwise rule means that if you drag the pointer from one pixel (or bit) on a template to another, the Auto Trace tool will draw a line that begins precisely on the first pixel, travels around the template in a clockwise direction, and ends precisely on the pixel on which you released the mouse button. If you click, drag, and release on the outside edge of a template, the path will be drawn clockwise around the outside.

5 Notice points 1 and 2 in the illustration below. Position the pointer at point 1 (within 2 pixels of the outside of the template). Hold down the

mouse button, drag the pointer to point 2, and release the mouse button. The Auto Trace tool will trace the section in a clockwise direction.

When using this feature, remember the Bits Clockwise rule. The Auto Trace tool always begins drawing its line clockwise around the template from the point at which you press and hold down the mouse button, and it ends the line at the point at which you release the mouse button.

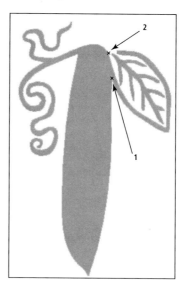

6 Select the Zoom-in tool, and click once near the top of the pea pod.

7 Select the Freehand tool, and finish drawing the pea pod. Be sure to begin drawing on an anchor point.

8 Choose Artwork Only from the View menu.

9 Choose Close from the File menu. Do not save changes.

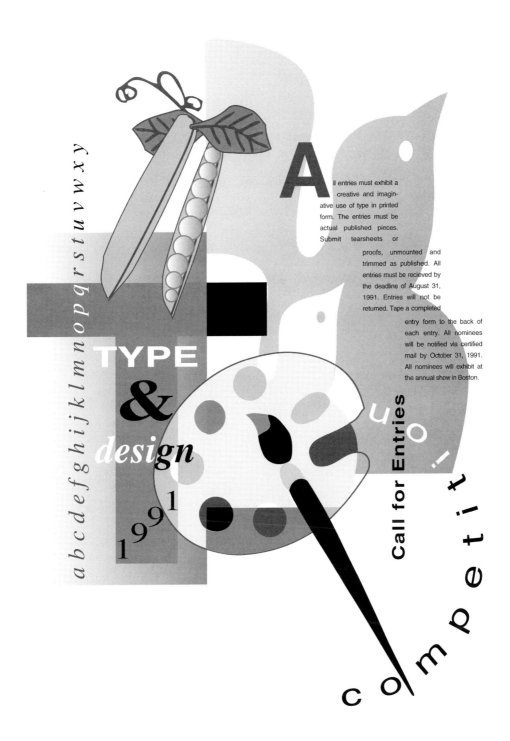

abcdefghijklmnopqrstuvwxy

TYPE

&

design

1991

All entries must exhibit a creative and imaginative use of type in printed form. The entries must be actual published pieces. Submit tearsheets or proofs, unmounted and trimmed as published. All entries must be recieved by the deadline of August 31, 1991. Entries will not be returned. Tape a completed entry form to the back of each entry. All nominees will be notified via certified mail by October 31, 1991. All nominees will exhibit at the annual show in Boston.

Call for Entries

competition!

Lesson

2

LESSON 2: USING OTHER DRAWING TECHNIQUES

There are four rectangle tools in the toolbox. They are the Rectangle, the Centered-rectangle, the Rounded-rectangle, and the Centered-rounded-rectangle tools.

Drawing rectangles visually

You can create rectangles of any proportion and perfect squares with the Rectangle tool.

1 Choose New from the File menu.

2 Choose Toolbox Options from the View menu, and choose Reset Toolbox from the submenu.

3 Choose Preferences from the Edit menu, click Inches under Ruler Units, and click OK.

4 Select the Rectangle tool.

5 Place the pointer at the top left corner of the screen, and hold down the mouse button. Then hold down the Shift key.

6 Drag the pointer diagonally down to the right, until the rectangle is approximately 2 inches by 2 inches, and then release the mouse button and the Shift key.

Note: Hold down the Shift key while you drag the pointer to make a perfect square; use the Centered-rectangle tool from the center.

Rectangle dialog box

You can make rectangles with given dimensions, as well as round-cornered rectangles and squares, with the Rectangle dialog box.

Note: Rectangles are grouped objects. You can edit parts of a rectangle by ungrouping it or by using the Direct-selection tool.

1 With the Rectangle tool selected, position the pointer in the center of the right side of screen.

2 Click the mouse button. (Do not drag.) The Rectangle dialog box will appear. Type 2 after Width, type 3 after Height, and click OK.

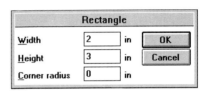

Rectangles with round corners

1 Select the Rounded-rectangle tool.

2 Click the mouse button. (Do not drag.) The Rectangle dialog box will appear. Type 2 after Width and 3 after Height.

3 Type .2 (two tenths) after Corner Radius, and click OK.

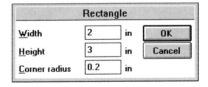

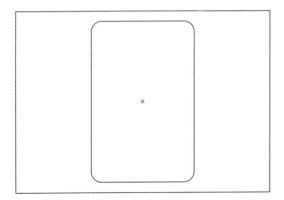

Note: The corner radius of rectangles can be set in the Preferences dialog box (discussed later) as well as in the Rectangle dialog box.

TIP: USE THE TAB
KEY TO MOVE THROUGH
THE DIALOG BOX.

OVAL TOOLS

The Oval tools work much as the Rectangle tools work. The ovals and circles you create are actually grouped objects consisting of two paths.

Drawing ovals visually

 You can create ovals of any proportion as well as perfect circles with the oval tools. There are two oval tools: the Oval tool and the Centered-oval tool.

Note: You can edit parts of an oval by ungrouping it or by using the Direct-selection tool.

1 Choose Select All from the Edit menu, and press the Delete or Backspace key to erase all the artwork in the current document.

2 Select the Oval tool.

3 Place the pointer at the top left corner of the screen, and hold down the mouse button. Also hold down the Shift key.

4 Drag the pointer diagonally down to the right, until the oval is approximately 2 inches by 2 inches, and then release the mouse button.

Oval dialog box

You can make oval shapes with specific measurements with the Oval dialog box.

1 With the Oval tool selected, position the pointer on the right side of the screen.

2 Click the mouse button. (Do not drag.) The Oval dialog box will appear. Type 3 after Width, type 1 after Height, and click OK.

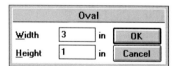

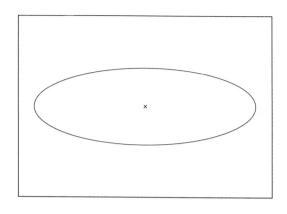

WORKING WITH GROUPED OBJECTS

Rectangles and ovals are automatically grouped, which means that if you select one point on the shape with the Selection tool (solid arrow), all the points are selected, making it easy to move them as units.

There are two ways to edit the individual points or segments of a grouped object. You can use the Direct-selection tool (hollow arrow), or you can ungroup the objects.

The program automatically groups certain objects (rectangles, ovals, and graphs, for example). In addition, you can use the Group command to group paths.

Note: There are multiple levels of grouping. If you have two objects that are grouped together and you group them with a third object, you must ungroup two times to have three ungrouped objects.

Using the Direct-selection tool

1 Choose Select All from the Edit menu, and press the Delete or Backspace key to clear the screen.

2 Select the Centered-rounded-rectangle tool, and click near the center of the window.

Watch the Status Line to see which tool is selected.

3 Type 2 for Width, 3 for Height, and .2 (two tenths) for Corner Radius. Click OK.

4 Choose the Selection tool (solid arrow) and click away from the artwork to deselect everything.

5 Use the Selection tool and click the edge of the rectangle. Notice that all points are selected because the object is grouped.

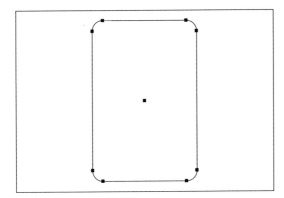

Note: Use the Selection tool when you want to select all parts of a grouped object.

6 Choose the Direct-selection tool (hollow arrow).

7 Click away from the artwork to deselect everything.

8 Click the edge of the rectangle. Notice that the entire grouped object is *not* selected when you use the Direct-selection tool.

Watch the Status Line to see which tool is selected.

9 Move the pointer to an anchor point and drag it.

Note: Use the Direct-selection tool when you want to select only a part of a grouped object.

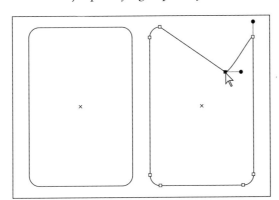

Using the Ungroup command

Use the Ungroup command when you no longer want objects to be grouped.

Whenever you ungroup an oval or a rectangle, you can delete the center point, unless you plan to use it later.

1 Choose the Selection tool (solid arrow).

2 Click the edge of the rectangle to select it.

3 Choose Ungroup from the Arrange menu.

4 Click away from the rectangle to deselect everything.

5 Click the center anchor point to select it.

6 Press the Delete or Backspace key to remove the center anchor point.

7 Position the pointer on a line segment and drag to move it.

8 Click a corner of the rectangle to select an anchor point.

9 Move the pointer to an anchor point and drag it.

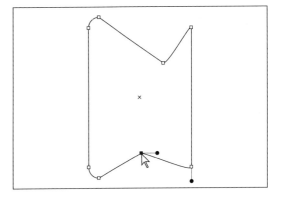

EDITING ANCHOR POINTS

Anchor points can edited in many ways. Several of the tools and techniques used in editing anchor points will be introduced below.

Splitting paths with the Scissors tool

The Scissors tool can be used to produce a break in a path. Cuts made with the Scissors tool must be on a line or a curve rather than on an endpoint.

1 Choose Select All from the Edit menu, and press the Backspace key to erase all the artwork in the document.

2 Choose Toolbox Options from the View menu, and Reset Toolbox from the submenu.

3 Select the Oval tool.

4 Hold down the Shift key, and drag to draw an oval about 2 inches by 2 inches in the center of the screen.

5 Choose Ungroup from the Arrange menu.

6 Choose the Selection tool and click off the oval to deselect it.

7 Select the Scissors tool. Notice that the Status Line reads "Split path" when the Scissors tool is selected.

8 Position the pointer at the top of the oval, and click the mouse button. You now have two anchor points, one on top of the other.

9 Position the pointer on the right side of the oval and click the mouse button. You have created two new anchor points that are not connected.

10 Choose the Object-selection tool (solid arrow with a +).

Note: Use the Object-selection tool to select all the points on a path.

11 Drag the top right segment of the oval. You see the selected endpoints of the path.

12 Drag the segment away from the oval.

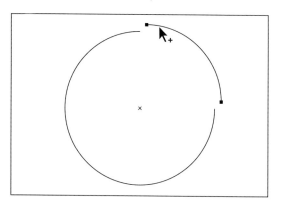

You can see that a segment has been removed from what was once a single path. You can use the Scissors tool to snip out any portion of an ungrouped path. You cannot cut an endpoint, because the Scissors tool creates endpoints.

Adding anchor points

You can use the Add-anchor-point tool to add an anchor point to an existing path without splitting the path.

1 Choose Select All from the Edit menu, and press the Delete or Backspace key to erase all the artwork in the document.

2 Select the Rectangle tool.

3 Hold down the Shift key, and drag to draw a square about 2 inches by 2 inches.

4 Select the Add-anchor-point tool. (The Add-anchor-point tool is in the toolbox next to the Scissors tool.)

Watch the Status Line to see which tool is selected.

5 Position the pointer at the center of the top line of the square, and click the mouse button. A new anchor point appears.

6 Click the center of each side of the square to add an anchor point on the other three sides.

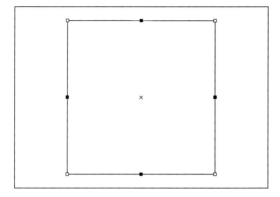

7 Choose the Direct-selection tool.

Note: *Use the Direct-selection tool to select anchor points that are part of grouped objects.*

8 Drag the anchor point at the center of the top segment down about halfway toward the center point.

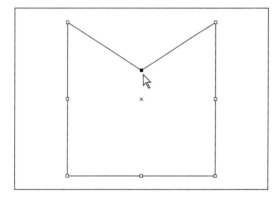

9 Drag the other anchor points in the center of each segment toward the center to make a star.

Converting direction points

 You can use the Convert-direction-point tool to convert corner points to smooth points.

1 Select the Convert-direction-point tool. The pointer changes to an open arrow.

Watch the Status Line to see which tool is selected.

2 Position the pointer on the top left anchor point of the star.

3 Hold down the mouse button and drag left and down. The anchor point is converted to a smooth point.

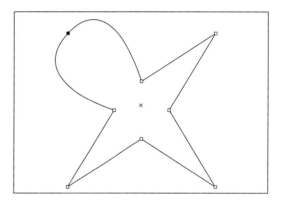

4 Position the pointer on the bottom left anchor point, and drag down and right.

5 Work your way around the star, dragging the remaining points of the star into smooth points until you have a four-leaf clover shape.

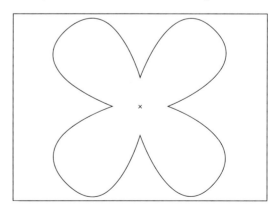

TIP: HOLDING DOWN THE SHIFT KEY WHEN YOU MOVE AN OBJECT CONSTRAINS MOVEMENT TO THE HORIZONTAL OR VERTICAL ANGLE.

You can also use the Convert-direction-point tool to convert smooth points to corner points.

6 Position the pointer on the top left anchor point of the four-leaf clover.

7 Click the mouse button. (Do not drag.) The anchor point is converted to a corner point.

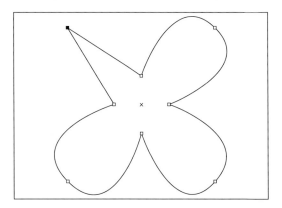

8 Click the remaining sides of the four-leaf clover shape to convert all the points back to corner points.

Deleting anchor points

 You can use the Delete-anchor-point tool to remove unwanted anchor points.

1 Choose the Delete-anchor-point tool.

2 Position the pointer on one of the inner anchor points of the shape, and click the mouse button. The anchor point is deleted.

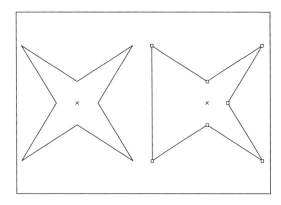

3 Click the remaining anchor points near the center of the star. The anchor points are deleted, and the shape returns to a square.

4 Click the top right corner of the square. The anchor point is deleted, and the shape becomes a right triangle.

5 Click to delete the point that was originally the center anchor point of the rectangle.

CREATING GUIDES

You can drag horizontal and vertical guides from the rulers to help you align objects and text. You also can use the Make Guide command in the Arrange menu to convert a graphic object into a guide to help you plan and arrange your artwork. A guide is displayed as a dotted line and is not printed.

When you use the Snap To feature (in the Preferences dialog box) with a guide, the pointer snaps to any part of the guide. When you snap to an object, the pointer turns hollow, and the Status Line indicates that you are snapping to an object.

Creating, moving, and deleting ruler guides

1 Choose Show Rulers from the View menu or press Control-R for the Show Rulers command.

2 Position the pointer inside the right ruler.

3 Hold down the mouse button and drag into the window.

4 Position the pointer in the bottom ruler and drag up to create a horizontal guide.

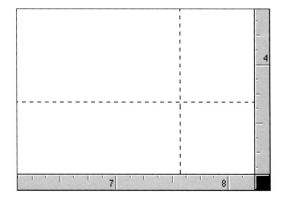

5 Choose the Selection tool.

6 Position the pointer on one of the guides you created.

7 Hold down the Shift key and the Control key, and drag the guide to a new location. Once you begin dragging, release the Shift and Control keys.

8 Position the pointer on one of the guides you created.

9 Hold down the Control and Shift keys, and double-click the guide to turn it to a line.

10 Press the Backspace key to delete the guide.

You can also delete a ruler guide by dragging it back into the ruler.

Converting graphic objects into guides

1 Using the Selection tool, click the edge of the triangle to select it.

2 Choose Make Guide from the Arrange menu or press Control-5 for the Make Guides command. The triangle is converted into a guide object.

3 Choose Release All Guides from the Arrange menu. The triangle guide is converted back into an artwork path.

PAINTING AND PREVIEWING

With the Adobe Illustrator program, you can print the objects in your artwork with black, white, shades of gray, patterns, and process or custom color.

Filling and stroking

1 Choose Select All from the Edit menu or press Control-A, and press the Backspace or Delete key to erase all the artwork in the document.

2 Use the Oval tool, with the Shift key, to draw a 2-inch circle on the left side of your screen.

3 Choose the Selection tool.

4 Begin to drag a copy of the circle about one-half inch to the right of the original circle. Hold down the Alternate key after you start to drag the shape to make a copy. Hold down the Shift key to constrain the copy to horizontal movement only.

5 Choose Transform Again from the Arrange menu or press Control-D for Transform Again command to create an additional copy. You should now have three circles.

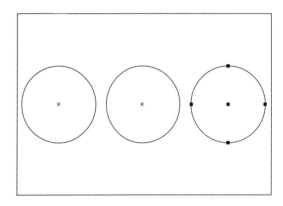

6 Use the Selection tool to select the circle in the center.

7 Choose Preview Illustration from the View menu or press Control-Y for the Preview Illustration command.

To see an approximation (or "preview") of what your artwork will look like when it is printed, including lines, shades of gray, and colors, use the Preview Illustration command. You can edit in Preview mode, although you will find the editing process slower in Preview mode because it takes more time to display previewed art. Artwork & Template mode, the mode you usually work in, displays both the background template and the drawn artwork.

8 Choose Paint Style from the Paint menu or press Control-I for the Paint Style command. The Paint Style dialog box will appear.

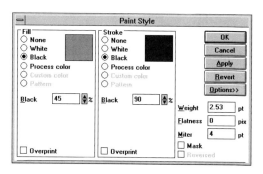

9 Select Black from the pop-up menu under Fill (if it is not already selected).

10 Double-click or drag to highlight the Black field, and type 45. (This fills the area inside the outline with 45 percent black.)

11 Select Black from the pop-up menu under Stroke.

12 Double-click or drag to highlight the Black field, and type 90. (This sets the shade or color of the outline.)

13 Double-click or drag to highlight the Weight field, and type 2.53.

Weight is the thickness of the stroke. It is always measured in points, regardless of the units of measurement selected in the Preferences dialog box. The stroke can be any weight from 0 to 1296 points. Up to two decimal places can be used to obtain exact line weights, such as 1.94 points, or a path can be assigned no stroke. Both the stroke and the fill can be given any shade of gray or any color.

14 Click Apply.

15 Click away from the artwork to deselect everything.

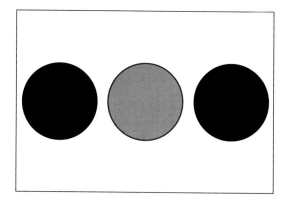

PAINTING WITH COLORS

In addition to specifying shades of gray, you can choose colors in the Paint Style dialog box.

Process color

The four primary ink colors used in printing full-color imagery are called process colors. They are cyan, magenta, yellow, and black (CMYK). By mixing certain percentages of these process colors, you can get an almost infinite number of colors.

If you have a color monitor, you can see the mixed colors in the Paint Style dialog box and in the previewed artwork. If you have a monochrome monitor, you will not be able to see any color—only representative shades of gray, but any color information you specify will still be contained in your illustration. This allows you to create color work for print without a color computer.

1 Using the Selection tool, click the edge of the rightmost circle.

2 Click the Paint Style dialog box near the bottom of the screen.

3 Choose Process Color under Fill, and type 100 for Magenta and 100 for Yellow. (This fills the area inside the outline with red.)

4 Choose Process Color under Stroke, and type 100 for Yellow to create a yellow outline. Type 4 for Weight, and click Apply.

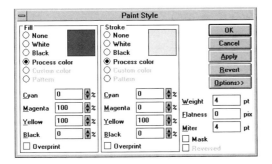

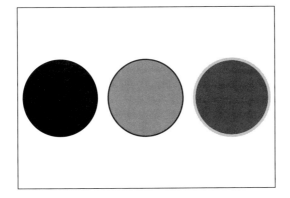

Note: If you are using a color monitor, the colors will appear on your screen. If you are using a monochrome monitor, the colors are displayed as shades of gray. The color information is still present in the file and can be printed on a color printer.

The default color settings are 100 percent black fill with no stroke. If you get unexpected results, check these settings.

Custom color

The custom color feature allows you to use the colors in the PANTONE® Process Color System, FOCOLTONE® COLOUR SYSTEM, TRU-MATCH™ color swatching system, and TOYO Ink Electronic Color Finder 1050 color standard set, as well as custom-mixed colors that you create. To specify a particular color standard shade, either

look it up in a specific color reference manual or view it on your color screen. You can then assign the color to fill and/or stroke a selected path, as you do with other tone and shade assignments.

To use the color standard sets of colors, you must first open the specific color document stored in the Adobe Illustrator directory, since the custom color information is stored in a saved document rather than in the Adobe Illustrator application. Do not create artwork in the color standard document.

Process color versus custom color

Process color is made up of four colors: cyan, magenta, yellow, and black (CMYK). The Adobe Separator™ program (included in the Adobe Illustrator package) is used to print these four colors on separate pieces of paper or film; they are then ready for printing on a four-color printing press. An object that has been painted red in the Adobe Illustrator program will appear on both the magenta page and the yellow page. At printing time, the magenta ink is printed on top of the yellow ink, creating red.

Custom color is based on a color standard. The color standards are recognized international standards for color, and are licensed as a part of the Adobe Illustrator program. These colors represent inks mixed to very specific standards set by the color standard companies such as PANTONE, FOCOLTONE, TRUMATCH, and Toyo, so that a 485 red printed in San Francisco will look exactly the same as a 485 red printed in Sydney, Australia. While this is a more expensive ink printing process than process color, it is much more accurate.

1 Leave the file with the circles open.

2 Choose Open from the File menu or press Control-O for the Open command. Select the file called *PANTONE.AI*, located in the *AI4* directory in a subdirectory called *COLOR*, and click Open.

TIP: USE THE RESIZE BAR, THE NARROW GRAY BORDER LINING THE BOTTOM OF THE WINDOW, TO CHANGE THE SIZE OF THE WINDOW. DRAG UP OR DOWN FROM THE CENTER OF THE BAR TO MAKE THE WINDOW TALLER OR SHORTER. DRAG RIGHT OR LEFT FROM EITHER END OF THE BAR TO MAKE THE WINDOW WIDER OR NARROWER.

Now that the PANTONE Colors file is open, the colors stored in that file can be used to color objects in any other window. Any or all of these colors can now be saved into another window as well. Once you have opened the file, you can select a path, display the Paint Style dialog box, and click Custom Color for the fill or stroke settings. When the PANTONE Color numbers appear, you can scroll down the list to find the one you want.

3 Choose Untitled art from the Window menu. This displays the window with the circles.

4 Select the leftmost circle.

5 Click the Paint Style dialog box.

6 Choose Custom Color under Fill.

7 Scroll and select PANTONE 321.

8 Choose Black under Stroke, and click OK.

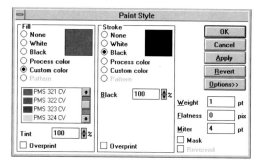

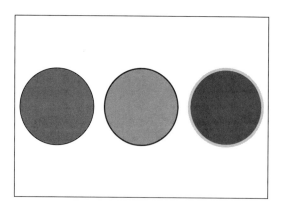

9 Choose Artwork Only from the View menu or press Control-W for the Artwork Only command.

10 Close all open files. Do not save changes.

LAYERING OBJECTS

As you create objects with the Adobe Illustrator program, the most recently created objects are placed in front of previously created objects, so that when you preview or print your illustration, these new shapes cover the previous ones. This is referred to as layering. *Layering* is like cutting out pieces of paper and laying them down on top of one another in a particular order to make a picture.

There are two ways to change the layering of objects. The first is to move a selected object in front or in back of everything else; the second is to selectively place an object in front or in back of another specific object.

Unlike other object-oriented design applications, the Adobe Illustrator program keeps layered paths in the order in which you lay them down; editing a path does not affect its layering order relative to the other objects in the illustration.

1 Choose Open from the File menu or press Control-O for the Open command.

2 Select the file called *LAYERART.AI*, located in the *ILLCIB* subdirectory in the directory called *AI4*.

Editing and previewing together

Although you can edit in Preview mode, you will probably do most of your editing in Artwork or Artwork & Template mode because of speed and memory considerations. In this lesson you edit while working in Preview Mode.

1 Scroll to move the artwork to the center of the window.

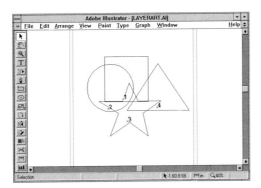

2 Choose Preview Illustration from the View menu or press Control-Y for the Preview Illustration command.

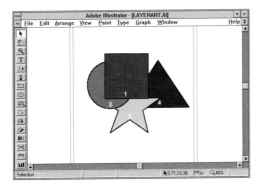

Using Paste In Front and Paste In Back

The file is layered with the square on the front layer. The next layer is the circle, and the next is the star. The triangle is on the back layer.

Suppose you want to put the square between the star and the triangle.

1 Choose the Selection tool.

2 Click to select the square.

3 Choose Cut from the Edit menu or press Control-X for the Cut command. This removes the square from the illustration and stores it on the clipboard.

4 Click to select the triangle.

5 Choose Paste In Front from the Edit menu or press Control-F for the Paste In Front command to retrieve the square and place it in front of the selected object (the triangle).

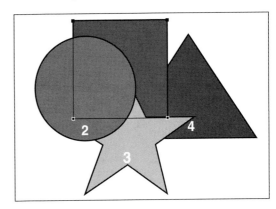

The file is now layered as follows: circle, star, square, triangle.

Next, suppose you want to place the circle between the square and the triangle.

1 Click to select the circle.

2 Choose Cut from the Edit menu or press Shift-Delete for the Cut command. This removes the circle from the illustration and stores it on the clipboard.

3 Click to select the square.

4 Choose Paste In Back from the Edit menu or press Control-B for the Paste In Back command to retrieve the circle from the clipboard and place it behind the selected object (the square).

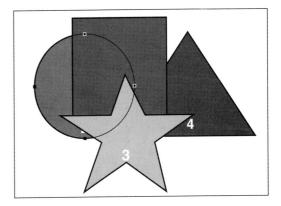

Using Bring To Front and Send To Back

You can use the Bring To Front and Send To Back commands to move a selection in front or in back of all the objects in an illustration, rather than placing it selectively in front or in back of a selected object.

The file is now layered as follows: star, square, circle, triangle.

Suppose you want to place the square on the top.

1 Click to select the square.

2 Choose Bring To Front from the Edit menu or press Control-T for the Bring To Front command. The square is now on top.

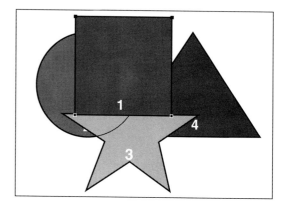

3 With the square selected, choose Send To Back from the Edit menu or press Control-Shift-B for the Send To Back command. This moves the square to the bottom layer.

4 Choose Close from the File menu. Do not save changes.

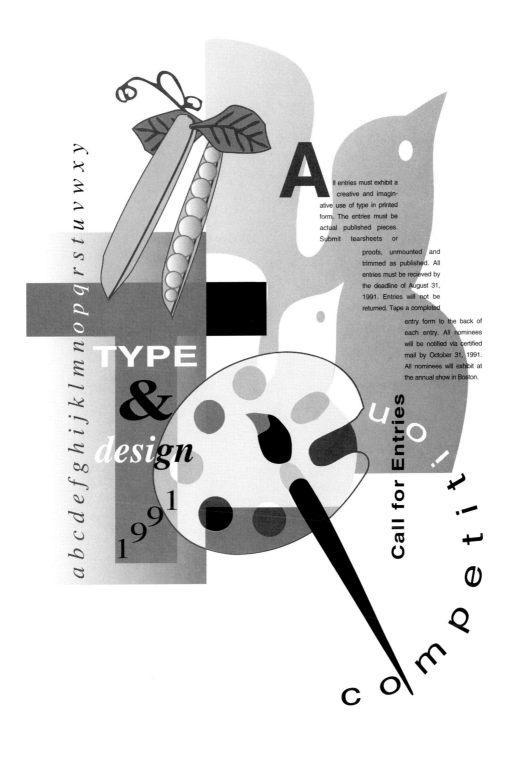

a b c d e f g h i j k l m n o p q r s t u v w x y

TYPE

&

design

1991

A

ll entries must exhibit a creative and imaginative use of type in printed form. The entries must be actual published pieces. Submit tearsheets or proofs, unmounted and trimmed as published. All entries must be recieved by the deadline of August 31, 1991. Entries will not be returned. Tape a completed entry form to the back of each entry. All nominees will be notified via certified mail by October 31, 1991. All nominees will exhibit at the annual show in Boston.

Call for Entries

competition!

Lesson

3

Lesson 3: Creating Type

With the Adobe Illustrator type tools, you can add type to any layout or illustration. A text object consists of a letter, a word, or several paragraphs. Text objects are treated as graphic objects. This means that all the actions that you perform on graphic objects including moving, copyong, deleting, transforming, grouping, and painting can be performed on text objects.

Viewing the Type Style Palette

1 Choose New from the File menu or press Control-N to open a new file.

There are three type tools: the Type tool, the Area-type tool, and the Path-type tool. Each type tool has its own pointer.

2 Choose Toolbox Options from the View menu, and Reset Toolbox from the submenu.

3 Select the Type tool. The pointer is an I-beam with a crosshair inside a dotted box. The crosshair shows the baseline of the type you will create.

4 Choose Type Style from the Type menu or press Control-T for the Type Style command.

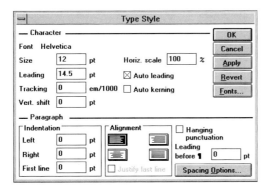

Font

The font pop-up menu lets you select any installed PostScript font.

Note: Many options in the Type Style dialog box can also be accessed directly from the Type menu or by using keyboard alternatives.

Exploring the Fonts dialog box

1 Click the Fonts button. The Font dialog box is brought up.

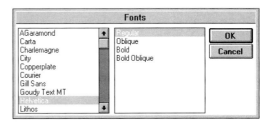

2 Scroll through the Family column and highlight Times.

3 Click to select Bold in the Typeface list.

4 Click OK once to close the Font dialog box. (The Type Style dialog box should still be open.)

Size

You can select any point size between 0.1 and 1296 points. (A point is 1/72 of an inch.)

Leading

Leading, the amount of space between baselines, is measured in points. You can change the units in the Type Preferences area of the Preferences dialog box. The default is 120 percent of the type size. For example, if the type size is 10, the leading defaults to 12.

Tracking/Kerning

Kerning refers to the amount of space between a pair of characters. Tracking refers to the amount of space between all selected characters. Use tracking to adjust the spacing of a word or an entire text object. Negative values move characters closer together. Positive values move characters apart.

Vert. shift

Vertical shift controls the distance that type appears from its baseline. You can raise or lower selected text.

Horiz. scale

Horizontal scale specifies the proportion between the height and width of the type. Unscaled characters have a value of 100 percent.

If you have scaled characters nonuniformly using a transformation tool, you can return them to their original proportions by setting the horizontal scale to 100 percent.

Auto leading

The default Auto leading option sets the leading at 120 percent of the font size.

Auto kerning

Many fonts contain information about the spacing of character pairs. If the Auto kerning option is on, the Adobe Illustrator program uses the kerning information contained in the font to space characters.

Indentation

Indentation specifies the amount of space between the path that contains text and the edge of the characters in each line of a text object. (You can also set a separate indentation for the first line of a paragraph.)

Alignment

Alignment controls how lines of type are arranged in paragraphs. Type can be aligned left, right, centered, or justified. The default is left aligned. You can also select whether or not to justify the last line of a paragraph (the default is not to justify the last line).

Hanging punctuation

Hanging punctuation controls whether punctuation marks fall inside or outside the text margins.

Leading before paragraph

This option controls the amount of space between the first line of a paragraph and the preceding paragraph.

Spacing options

Spacing options control the word and letter spacing in lines of type.

You can close the Type Style dialog box by clicking the close button in the upper right corner of the dialog box, or you can leave the dialog box open, and drag it out of the way of your document.

5 Click OK to close the Type Style dialog box.

CREATING TYPE AT A SPECIFIED POINT

By selecting the Type tool and positioning it on the page and clicking, you specify the point at which text will appear once typed in on the keyboard.

Entering text on the page

1 Use the Type tool, click and release on the screen, and type the following:

Home is where the heart is

2 Select the text by dragging through it, or click the text, and press Control-A to select the entire paragraph.

3 Choose Type Style from the Type menu.

4 Type **36** for Size and click the Centered Alignment icon.

TIP: PRESS ALTERNATE-LEFT ARROW WITH THE INSERTION POINT BETWEEN TWO CHARACTERS TO MOVE THEM CLOSER TOGETHER. PRESS ALTERNATE-RIGHT ARROW TO MOVE THEM APART. USE CONTROL-ALTERNATE-LEFT/RIGHT ARROW TO MOVE FIVE TIMES THE KERNING VALUE.

5 If necessary, drag the Type Style dialog box aside so you can see your text.

6 Click Apply to see the changes.

7 Click Size in the Type Style dialog box, type **24.7** for Size, and click Apply.

8 Click on the screen, drag to select the H at the beginning of the text.

9 Click Size in the Type Style dialog box, type **78** for Size, and click OK.

10 Hold down the Alternate and Shift keys and press the Right Arrow key to increase the font size, or the left arrow key to decrease the font size.

Watch the Status Line to see the font and size of selected type.

Adjusting kerning

1 Click between the *w* and the *h* in *where*.

2 Hold down the Alternate key and use the Left Arrow key on the keyboard to decrease the kerning and move the two characters closer together.

Home is where the heart is

3 Click between the words *where* and *the*, and press the Enter key.

4 Drag to select both lines of text.

5 Choose Alignment from the Type menu and Right from the submenu, or press Control-Shift-R to align text to the right.

Adjusting the leading

1 Hold down the Alternate key and press the Up/Down Arrow keys to change the leading.

2 Drag to select only the *H* in *Home*.

3 Hold down the Alternate and Shift keys and press the Down Arrow key several times to create a drop cap.

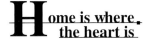

4 Choose the Selection tool, and select the text object from the previous exercise.

5 Press the Delete or Backspace key to delete the text object.

CREATING TYPE IN AN AREA

Type may also be created so that it fits in the boundaries of a shape such as a rectangle. Text can be typed or imported into a shape.

Creating text objects and importing text

1 Select the Type tool and drag a rectangle about 2 inches by 4 inches near the left side of the screen.

2 Choose Type Style from the Type menu.

3 Click Size in the Type Style dialog box, and type **12** for Size.

4 Click Auto Leading in the Type Style dialog box.

5 Click Kerning, and change the value to **0**.

6 Click Vert. Shift, and change the value to **0**.

7 Click the Left Alignment icon.

8 Click OK.

TIP: USE THE DIRECT-
SELECTION TOOL TO
EDIT THE PATHS OF
TEXT OBJECTS.

9 Choose Import from the File menu and choose Text from the submenu. Click the file named *QQTXT.SAM*, and click Open.

A stitch in time saves nine. All good things come to those who wait. Too many cooks spoil the broth. I have seen the future, and it works. The early bird catches the worm. A bird in the hand is worth tow in the bush. Don't beat a dead horse. Don't burn the candle from both ends. There's got to be a pony in there somewhere. A penny saved is a penny earned. Don't cross your bridges before you come to them. Don't be penny wise and pound foolish. There are three kinds of lies: lies, damned lies and statistics. Home is where the heart is. Early to bed, early to rise makes a man

Linking text objects

1 Click the Type tool in the toolbox.

2 Drag to create a second rectangle about half the size of the first rectangle on the right of the original.

3 Choose the Selection tool, hold down the Shift key, and click the edge of the first rectangle so that both rectangles are selected.

4 Choose Link from the Type menu or press Control-Shift-G to Link. The text flows into the new text object.

5 Select the Oval tool.

6 Drag to draw an oval about 2 inches in diameter, below the two rectangles.

7 Choose the Selection tool, hold down the Shift key, and click the edge of one of the rectangles to select the linked rectangles.

8 Choose Link from the Type menu to link the rectangle and the oval. The text flows into the oval.

Note that when the oval was a graphic object, it contained a center anchor point. When you linked it with the text objects, the oval became a text object without a center anchor point.

9 Choose the Direct-selection tool and click away from the text objects to deselect everything.

10 Click the left edge of the left rectangle to select it.

11 Drag the bottom left anchor point of the left rectangle down to change the shape. The text automatically follows the new shape.

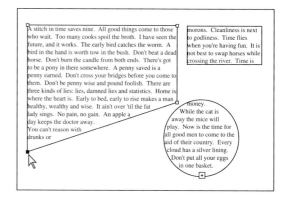

12 Use the Direct-selection tool to move different anchor points in the text objects.

Changing text attributes

1 Choose Toolbox Options from the View menu, and Reset Toolbox from the submenu.

2 Select the Type tool.

3 Click inside one of the text objects.

4 Choose Select All from the Edit menu.

5 Choose Type Style from the Type menu.

6 Press Alternate-F for the Font dialog command or click the Font button to bring up the Fonts .

7 Choose Adobe Garamond for Font, and click OK.

8 Type **18** for Size.

9 Make sure that Auto Leading is on.

10 Click the word *Tracking* to reset the value to **0**.

11 Click the words *Vert. Shift* to reset the value to **0**.

12 Click the Left Alignment icon, and click OK.

Painting text objects

1 Choose Paint Style from the Paint menu or press Control-I for the Paint Style command.

2 Choose Process Color under Fill. Type **100** for Cyan and **50** for Magenta, and click OK.

3 Choose Preview Illustration from the View menu.

4 Choose Artwork Only from the View menu or press Control-W for the Artwork Only command.

5 Choose the Direct-selection tool, and click outside the text object to deselect it.

6 Hold down the Shift key, and click the top edge of the text objects.

7 Choose Paint Style from the Paint menu.

8 Choose Process Color under Fill, and type **30** for Cyan.

9 Choose Black under Stroke, and click OK.

10 Choose Preview Illustration from the View menu or press Control-Y for the Preview Illustration command.

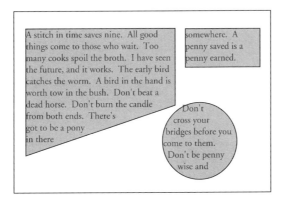

WRAPPING TEXT AROUND AN OBJECT

First you will create a graphic object, and then you will make the text wrap around that object.

Creating a graphic object

1 Select the Oval tool, position the pointer at the edge of the text objects, and click the mouse button.

2 Type **1** for Width, type **1** for Height, and click OK.

3 Choose Paint Style from the Paint menu.

4 Choose Process Color under Fill, type **50** for Magenta, None for Stroke, and click OK.

Making text wrap

1 Choose the Selection tool.

2 Hold down the Shift key and click the rectangle so that both the rectangle and the oval are selected.

3 Choose Make Text Wrap from the Type menu.

4 Choose the Direct-up selection tool, and click away from the text objects to deselect them.

5 Click the edge of the circle inside the text object.

6 Drag the circle to a different place in the text, hold down the Alternate key, and release the mouse button to make a copy.

7 Choose Artwork Only from the View menu.

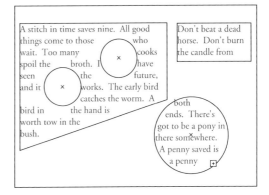

Using discretionary hyphens

1 Locate the word *somewhere* in the text.

2 Select the Type tool.

3 Position the pointer between the *e* and the *w* in *somewhere*, and click the mouse button.

4 Press Control-Shift-Keypad Hyphen. This enters a discretionary hyphen in the word *somewhere*.

Note: *The keypad Hyphen key must be used for discretionary hyphens.*

5 Choose the Direct-selection tool.

6 Hold down the Alternate key and double-click the copy of the circle to select the entire circle.

7 Drag the circle to different positions in the text object.

Notice the word *somewhere*. When there is not enough room, the word is hyphenated. When there is enough room, the hyphen does not show.

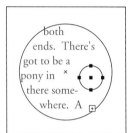 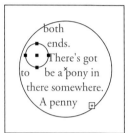

8 Choose Close from the File menu. Do not save changes.

CREATING TYPE ON AN OPEN PATH

Text can be entered on a path created with the Pen or Freehand tools. Once the text is entered on the path, the text can be repositioned along the curve. The path itself can also be altered.

1 Choose Open from the File menu or press Control-O for the Open command, and double-click the file named *PATHTL.AI*.

2 Scroll until the path is near the top of the screen.

3 Select the Type tool.

4 Move the pointer near the leftmost anchor point of the path, and click the mouse button.

5 Type the following:

Birds fly and do somersaults

6 Choose Select All from the Edit menu.

7 Choose Type Style from the Type menu or press Control-T for the Type Style command.

8 If necessary, move the Type Style dialog box so you can see the text.

9 Click the Fonts button.

10 Choose Poplar for Font, and click OK. Move the Type Style menu. Click the Fonts button and sample another typeface and click OK in the Font dialog.

11 In the Type Style dialog box, type **58** for Size, and click Apply.

12 Try other type sizes, until you find a size that fits the path. Click Apply to see how different sizes look, and when you have a right size click OK.

Moving the text alog the curve.

1 Choose the Direct-selection tool, and click away from the text to deselect everything.

2 Click the line, and drag an anchor point to move it. Move other anchor points.

3 Choose the Selection tool and click the curve to select it.

4 Position the pointer on the top of the type handle (the long I-beam) at the beginning of the text, and slowly drag to the right.

5 Drag the type handle down, below the curve.

6 Choose Select All from the Edit menu, and press the Delete or Backspace key to clear the screen.

CREATING TYPE ON A CIRCLE

You can bind type to any path and then edit the path separately.

Creating type on a path

1 Select the Centered-oval tool, click in the center of the left side of the window, type **3** for Width, type **3** for Height, and click OK.

2 Select the Path-type tool.

3 Move the pointer to the top of the circle, and click the mouse button.

4 Type the following:

A Rolling Stone Gathers No Moss

5 Choose Select All from the Edit menu.

6 Choose Type Style from the Type menu or press Control-T for the Type Style command. Drag the Type Style dialog box aside so that you can see both the dialog box and the circle.

7 Click Fonts and choose GillSans for Font.

8 Type **25** for Size.

9 Click the Centered Alignment icon, move the Type Style dialog box so you can see the text on your screen, and click Apply. The type is centered from the place where you clicked at the top of the circle.

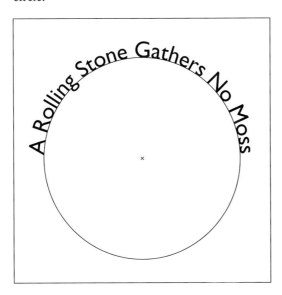

10 Type **-10** for Vert. Shift, and click Apply. The text is moved over the edge of the circle.

11 Type **-25** for Vert. Shift, and click Apply. This shifts the text to the inside of the circle.

12 Click the words *Vert. Shift* to return the value to the default of 0, and click Apply. This shifts the text back to the outside of the circle.

13 Click OK to close the Type Style dialog box.

Painting and editing the path

1 Choose the Direct-selection tool.

2 Click away from the text to deselect everything.

3 Click the bottom of the oval.

4 Choose Paint Style from the Paint menu.

5 Click Process Color for Fill.

6 Double-click in the color swatch next to Fill. The Choose Color dialog box appears. Press the mouse in the color area and select a yellow value, click OK, and then click OK in the Paint Style dialog box.

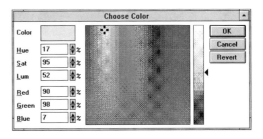

If you visually select a color using the color picker, you select a color from the RGB (red, green, and blue) color model; the color is then displayed as its cyan, magenta, yellow, and black equivalents. Using the color picker, you can choose the color's percentage of red, green, and blue, and its percentage of *hue*, *saturation*, and *luminosity*. Hue is the position of color in the color spectrum. Saturation measures the purity of the color. Luminosity measures the brightness of color.

When the color picker is displayed, you can scroll through a document and read the current fill or stroke attributes of an object and change them dynamically.

7 Click away from the artwork to deselect everything.

8 Choose Preview Illustration from the View menu.

9 Choose the Selection tool and click the oval.

10 Drag the type handle across the path toward the center of the oval.

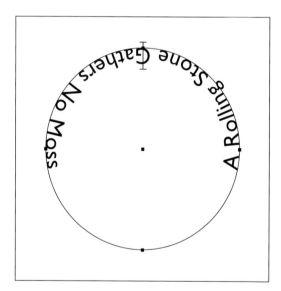

11 Close the file. Do not save changes.

CONVERTING TEXT OBJECTS TO PATH OUTLINES

When type is converted to outlines, the type is changed into a set of artwork paths that you can edit and manipulate as you would a graphic object. You can modify the outlines to make logos, paint them, or fill them with patterns. Type that has been turned into outlines cannot be changed back to type objects. If you are converting a lot of text to outlines, check the spelling, tracking, kerning, and leading before you convert.

Creating type outlines

1 Choose New from the File menu.

2 Select the Type tool and click the mouse button in the middle of the page.

3 Type the word **Type**, with a capital *T*.

4 Double-click the word to select it.

5 Choose Type Style from the Type menu.

6 Click Fonts, choose Times-bold for the font, and click OK.

7 Type **200** for size, and click OK.

8 Click any tool in the toolbox to select the entire text object.

9 Choose Create Outlines from the Type menu. The type is transformed into graphic objects.

10 Choose the Direct-selection tool.

11 Drag a selection marquee across the crossbar of the *T* to select only the crossbar.

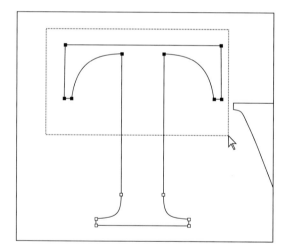

12 Position the pointer on the top edge of the *T*, and drag upward about 2 inches, holding down the Shift key to constrain the move.

13 Use the Direct-selection tool to select and move other parts of the letters.

14 Close all open files. Do not save changes.

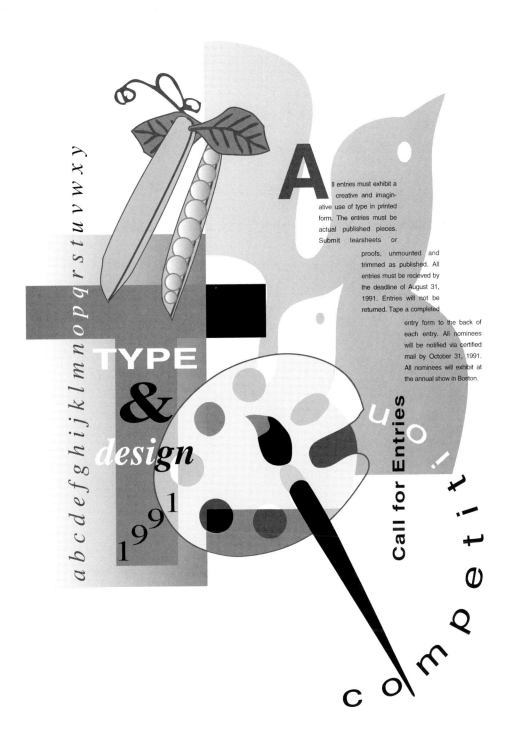

A

ll entries must exhibit a
creative and imagin-
ative use of type in printed
form. The entries must be
actual published pieces.
Submit tearsheets or

proofs, unmounted and
trimmed as published. All
entries must be recieved by
the deadline of August 31,
1991. Entries will not be
returned. Tape a completed

entry form to the back of
each entry. All nominees
will be notified via certified
mail by October 31, 1991.
All nominees will exhibit at
the annual show in Boston.

abcdefghijklmnopqrstuvwxy

TYPE

&

design

1991

Call for Entries

competition!

Lesson

4

Lesson 4: Dove Poster

This lesson is a directed study project designed to give you an opportunity to work on your own to practice the techniques you learned in lessons 1–3. The goal of special projects is to give you the time to apply the tools and techniques you have learned in the previous lessons.

In this lesson you will create this poster.

You will begin by creating and painting the rectangle that is the background. Then you will create the type for the title. You will create the dove artwork with the Auto Trace tool and paste it into the document. Finally, you will import text and make the text wrap around the artwork.

1 Choose New from the File menu.

2 Choose Place Template and double-click the file called *DOVETMP.TIF.*

3 Choose Preferences from the Edit menu, and set the Ruler Units to Picas/Points.

4 Choose Toolbox Options from the View menu and Reset Toolbox from the submenu.

Dove Poster Template

Drawing and painting the rectangle

1 Select the Rectangle tool.

2 Position the pointer on point A, and click the mouse button.

3 Type **364** for Width, type **506** for Height, and click OK.

4 Press Control-I for the paint style command and set the paint attributes as follows:

Fill: Process Color, M-20, Y-10
Stroke: None

5 Choose Actual Size from the View menu.

CREATING TYPE AND SETTING TYPE ATTRIBUTES

The type for the title will be created in two processes. You will first create and adjust the title, *Mother*. Then you will create and adjust type on a path to add the word *LOVE*.

Creating type

1 Select the Type tool.

2 Position the pointer on point C, and click the mouse button.

3 Type the word **Mother**.

Setting type attributes

1 Select the entire word *Mother*.

2 Choose Type Style from the Type menu or press Control-T for the Type Style command.

3 Choose Times-Bold for Font.

4 Type **95** for Size.

5 Make sure that Auto Leading is on.

6 Make sure that Auto Kerning is off.

7 Click the Centered Alignment icon, and click OK.

8 Set the paint attributes as follows:

Fill: Process Color, C-45, M-30, Y-0, K-10
Stroke: None

9 Using the Type tool, drag to select the *M*.

10 Choose Type Style from the Type menu.

11 Click Size, and type **120** for Size.

12 Type **-10** for Vert. Shift.

13 Type **80** for Horiz. Scale, and click OK.

Creating and editing type outlines

1 Choose the Selection tool.

When you select any other tool from the toolbox after you have created type, the entire text object becomes selected. You see the alignment point and the baseline when the object is selected.

2 Choose Create Outlines from the Type menu.

3 Choose Group from the Arrange menu or press Control-G for the Group command.

4 Choose the Direct-selection tool.

5 Position the pointer on point D, and drag up and left toward point A, to select the points shown in the figure.

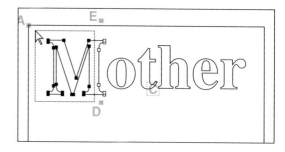

TIP: SET VERT. SHIFT TO 0 BY CLICKING THE WORD RATHER THAN BY ENTERING A VALUE IN THE FIELD.

6 Press the Left Arrow key on the keyboard 15 times, to expand the right leg of the M.

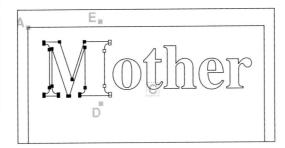

CREATING AND EDITING TYPE ON A PATH

First you draw a straight-line path with the Pen tool, and then you add type to that path.

To create type on a path

1 Select the Pen tool.

2 Position the pointer on point D, and click the mouse button.

3 Position the pointer on point E, hold down the Shift key, and click the mouse button.

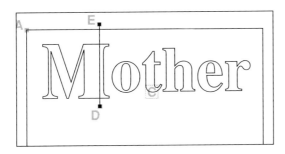

4 Select the Type tool.

5 Position the pointer on point D, and click the mouse button.

The pointer changes to the Path-type pointer when you move it over the line.

6 Type **LOVE** in all capitals.

Because the last font size you set was quite large, the letters will not all be seen on the screen.

Adjusting the type style

1 Choose Select All from the Edit menu.

2 Choose Type Style from the Type menu or press Control-T for the Type Style command.

3 Type **24** for Size.

4 Make sure that Auto Leading is on.

5 Click the words *Vert. Shift* to set the value to the default of 0.

6 Set the *Horiz. Scale* value to **100**, and click OK.

Adjustung the location and painting the type

1 Select any tool in the toolbox. This selects the entire text object.

2 Press the Up Arrow key on the keyboard to adjust the word *LOVE* until it is vertically centered in the leg of the *M*.

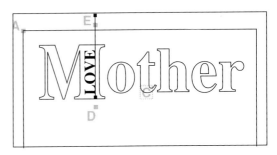

3 Select the Type tool, and double-click to select the word *LOVE*.

4 Choose Paint Style from the Paint menu or press Control-I for the Paint Style command.

5 Choose White under Fill, and click OK.

6 Choose Preview Illustration from the View Menu.

7 Choose Artwork & Template from the View Menu.

8 Choose Save As from the File menu.

9 Type **DOVSTUD.AI**, and click Save.

Note: In DOS/Windows, application filenames can be no longer than eight characters followed by the application suffix, which in this case is .AI.

Creating a text object and importing text

1 Select the Rectangle tool.

2 Click in the middle of the window to access the Rectangle dialog box.

3 Type **132** for Width and **345** for Height. Make sure that the Corner Radius is 0, and click OK.

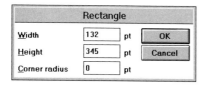

4 Scroll down until you can see point F and the bottom of the rectangle you just created.

5 Choose the Selection tool.

6 Position the pointer on the bottom right anchor point of the rectangle you just created, and drag to point F, to align the rectangle.

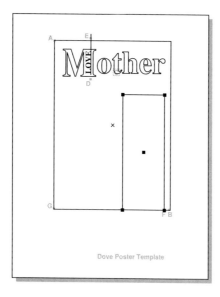

7 Select the Type tool.

8 Position the pointer on the edge of the rectangle you just moved, and click the mouse button. You will see an insertion point at the top of the rectangle.

9 Choose Import from the File menu and Text from the submenu, and double-click the file called *DOVETXT.SAM.*

Setting type attributes and painting type

1 Choose Select All from the Edit menu or press Control-A for the Select All command to select all of the imported text.

2 Choose Type Style from the Type menu.

3 Choose Helvetica-Regular for Font.

4 Type **20** for Size.

5 Type **36** for Leading.

6 Type **-50** for Tracking.

7 Type **100** for Horiz. Scale.

8 Under Indentation, type **10** for Left.

9 Click the Left Alignment icon, and click OK.

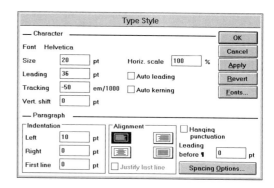

10 Set the paint attributes as follows:

Fill: White
Stroke: None

11 Choose Preview Illustration from the View menu or press Control-Y for the Preview Illustration command. Review the results.

Notice that there is a missing comma after *crafts*. Also, the *d* in *day* should be a capital.

12 Select the Type tool.

13 Drag to select the *d* in *day*, and change it to a capital.

14 Click after the word *crafts*, and add a comma.

15 Click after the word *music*, and add a period.

16 Choose Artwork and Template from the View menu.

17 Choose Save from the File menu.

ADDING GRAPHIC OBJECTS

Next you will auto trace and paint graphic objects from another file, and copy them into the current file. Finally, you will make the text wrap around the graphic objects.

Auto tracing and painting the doves

You create the graphics by auto tracing the doves from another file, then painting and editing them.

1 Choose New from the File menu.

2 Choose Place Template, double-click the file called *DOVETMP.TIF*, and click Place.

3 Select the Auto Trace tool.

4 Position the pointer on the curve of the upper wing of the large dove, and click the mouse button.

5 Set the paint attributes as follows:

   Fill: Process Color, C-30, M-20, Y-0

6 Position the pointer on the curve of the upper wing of the small dove, and click the mouse button.

7 Set the paint attributes as follows:

Fill: Process Color, C-20, M-12, Y-0

8 Select the Zoom-in tool, and click once in the screen.

9 Using the Auto Trace tool, click the edge of the eye of the large dove.

10 Click the edge of the eye of the small dove.

11 Choose the Object-selection tool.

12 Click to select one eye, hold down the Shift key, and click to select the other eye.

13 Choose Paint Style from the Paint menu.

14 Choose White under Fill, and click Apply.

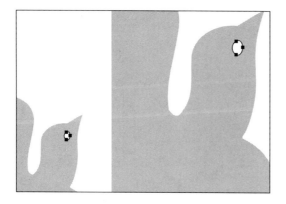

15 Choose Preview Illustration from the View menu.

16 Choose Artwork & Template from the View menu.

17 Select the Zoom-out tool and click once.

Copying the graphic objects into another file

1 Using the Object-selection tool, click away from the artwork to deselect everything.

2 Click the edge of the large dove. Hold down the Shift key and click the eye of the large dove.

3 Choose Group from the Arrange menu or press Control-G for the Group command.

4 Choose Copy from the Edit menu.

5 Choose DOVSTUD.AI:Dove Poster Template from the Window menu.

6 Choose Paste from the Edit menu or press Control-V for the Paste command. The dove is pasted into the file.

7 Select the Zoom-out tool and click once.

8 Choose the Selection tool.

9 Position the pointer on the bottom left anchor point of the dove, and drag until the anchor point is aligned with point G at the lower left corner of the page.

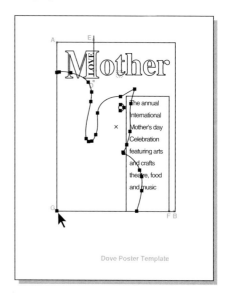

10 Choose Untitled art: Dove Template from the Window menu.

11 Repeat steps 1 through 9 for the small dove.

12 Choose Preview Illustration from the View menu.

13 Choose Artwork & Template from the View menu.

Making the text wrap

1 Using the Object-selection tool, click the edge of the large dove to select it.

2 Hold down the Shift key, and click the text object to the right of the large dove to add the text object to the selection.

3 Choose Make Text Wrap from the Type menu.

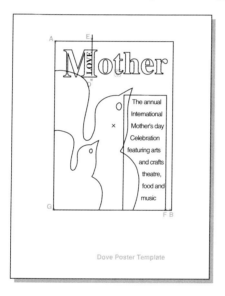

4 Click the *M* in *Mother*. Hold down the Shift key, and click the baseline of the word *LOVE*.

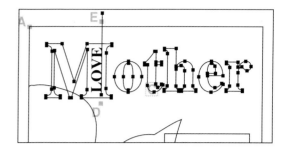

5 Choose Bring To Front from the Edit menu or press Control-Shift-T for the Bring To Front command. This moves the title in front of the large dove.

6 Choose Preview Illustration from the View menu.

7 Choose Save from the File menu.

8 Choose Print from the File menu, if a printer is available.

9 Choose Close from the File menu to close all files. Do not save changes.

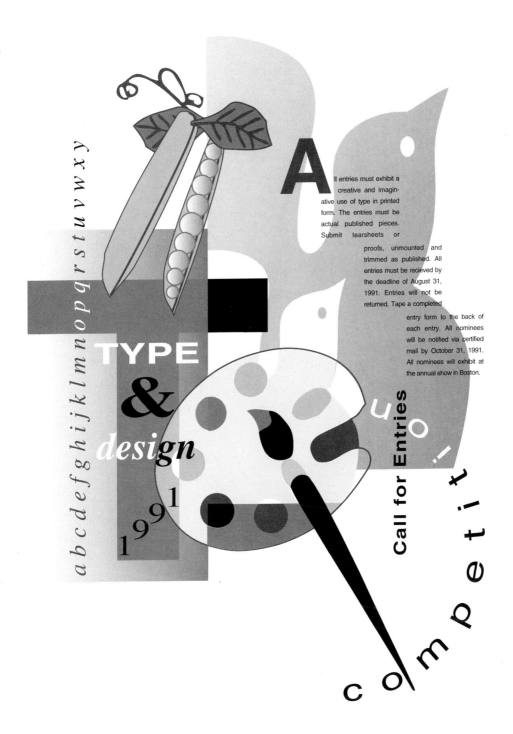

abcdefghijklmnopqrstuvwxy

TYPE

&

design

1 9 9 1

All entries must exhibit a creative and imaginative use of type in printed form. The entries must be actual published pieces. Submit tearsheets or proofs, unmounted and trimmed as published. All entries must be recieved by the deadline of August 31, 1991. Entries will not be returned. Tape a completed entry form to the back of each entry. All nominees will be notified via certified mail by October 31, 1991. All nominees will exhibit at the annual show in Boston.

Call for Entries

competition

Lesson

5

LESSON 5: TYPE POSTCARD

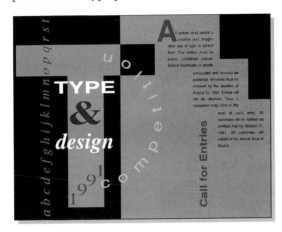

This lesson provides a project that you can use to practice the techniques you learned in lessons 1–3. You'll draw the promotional Type postcard below.

1 Choose New from the File menu.

2 Select the Zoom-out tool. Click once to zoom out.

3 Choose Print Setup from the File menu, click Landscape, and click OK.

4 Choose Place Template from the File menu, and double-click the file named *POSTTMP.TIF.*

5 Choose Preferences from the Edit menu or press Control-K for the Preference command, and set the Ruler Units to Picas/Points.

6 Choose Toolbox Options from the View menu, and Reset Toolbox from the submenu.

Take a moment to examine the template.

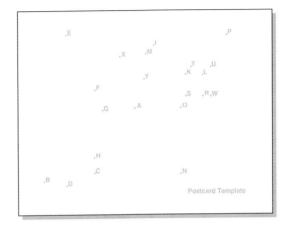

Postcard Template

Drawing and painting the larger rectangles

1 Choose Actual Size from the View menu.

2 Select the Centered-rectangle tool.

3 Position the pointer on point A, near the center of the drawing, and click the mouse button.

4 Type **570** for Width, **440** for Height, and **0** for Corner Radius, and click OK. This creates a large box for the border.

5 Press Control-I for the Paint Style command and set the paint attributes as follows:

Fill: Process Color, C-0, M-75, Y-75, K-20
Stroke: None

Note: Use the Tab and Arrow keys to move quickly through the Paint Style dialog box.

Drawing and painting the small rectangle

1 Using the Centered-rectangle tool, click again on point A.

2 Type **237** for Width and **440** for Height, and click OK.

3 Select the Zoom-out tool, and click once in the screen.

4 Choose the Selection tool.

5 Position the pointer on the bottom left anchor point of the small rectangle.

6 Drag the small rectangle until the bottom left corner is aligned with point B, press the Shift key, and release the mouse button.

7 Choose Paint Style from the Paint menu.

8 Choose Black under Fill, and click OK.

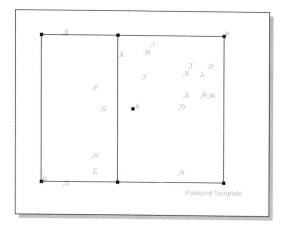

9 Choose Preview Illustration from the View menu.

10 Choose Artwork & Template from the View menu or press Control-E for the Artwork & Template command.

Creating type and setting type attributes

1 Select the Type tool.

2 Position the pointer on point C, click the mouse button, and type a capital **T**.

3 Drag to select the *T*.

4 Choose Type Style from the Type menu or press Control-T for the Type Style command.

5 Choose Helvetica-Bold for Font.

6 Type **480** for Size.

7 Click the word *Tracking* to restore the default value of 0.

8 Type **110** for Horiz. Scale.

9 Under Indentation, change the value for Left to **0**.

10 Click the Centered Alignment icon, and click OK.

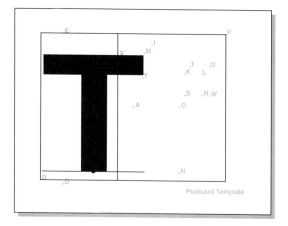

Creating the large T type outline

1 Choose the Selection tool.

When you click another tool after creating type, the text object is selected and you see the alignment point and the baseline.

2 Choose Create Outlines from the Type menu. The *T* is converted into artwork.

3 Choose Release Compound from the Paint menu. (This feature will be explained in a later lesson.)

4 Choose the Direct-selection tool.

5 Click away from the artwork to deselect it.

6 Click the top edge of the *T* to show the anchor points.

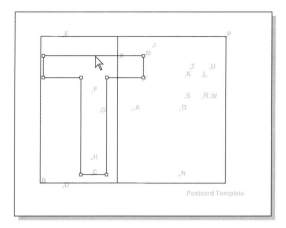

7 Press the Up Arrow key on the keyboard six times.

8 Choose Paint Style from the Paint menu or press Control-I for the Paint Style command.

9 Choose Black under Fill, type **70**, and click OK.

Creating a rectangle for the T

1 Select the Rectangle tool.

2 Position the pointer on point X, exactly on the corner, and drag down and right to point Y, exactly on the corner.

3 Choose Paint Style from the Paint menu.

4 Choose Black under Fill, and type **100**. Click OK.

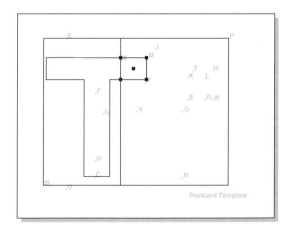

5 Choose Preview Illustration from the View menu.

6 Choose Artwork & Template from the View menu.

7 Choose Save As from the File menu.

8 Type **POSTSTUD.AI**, and click Save.

Creating and editing the alphabet on a path

1 Select the Pen tool.

2 Position the pointer on point D at the bottom of the page, and click the mouse button.

3 Hold down the Shift key, and click point E at the top of the page, to create a straight line.

4 Select the Type tool.

5 Position the pointer on point D. The pointer should be an I-beam with a jagged crosshair.

6 Click the mouse button.

Modifying the type style of the text

1 Choose Type Style from the Type menu or press Control-T for the Type Style command.

2 Choose Times-Italic for Font.

3 Type **30** for Size.

4 Make sure that Auto Leading is on.

5 Type **-9.5** for Vert. Shift.

6 Type **100** for Horiz. Scale.

7 Click the Left Alignment icon.

8 Click the Spacing Options button.

9 Type **115** for Desired Letter Spacing. Be sure to choose Letter Spacing, not Word Spacing.

10 Click OK to close the Spacing Options dialog box, and then click OK in the Type Style dialog box.

Typing and painting the alphabet

1 Type the alphabet (**a–z**) in lower-case letters. You may not see all the letters on the screen.

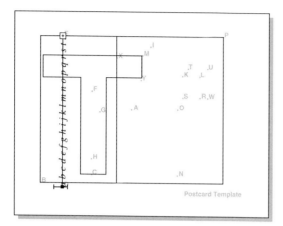

2 Choose Select All from the Edit menu.

When you have a blinking insertion point in a path and you choose Select All, all of the type in the path is selected.

Make sure that you have not selected any artwork, only type.

3 Choose Paint Style from the Paint menu or press Control-I for the Paint Style command.

4 Choose Black under Fill, type **75**, and click OK.

5 Choose the Direct-selection tool, and click away from the artwork to deselect it.

6 Click point D, and press the Up Arrow key so that only three letters are positioned inside the crossbar of the *T*, and the *a* is inside the bottom line of the box.

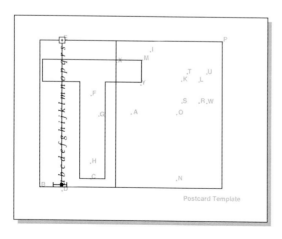

7 Select the Type tool.

8 Drag the I-beam pointer to select only the three letters that are inside the crossbar of the *T.*

9 Set the paint attributes as follows:

Fill: Process Color, M-75, Y-75, K-20

10 Choose Preview Illustration from the View menu.

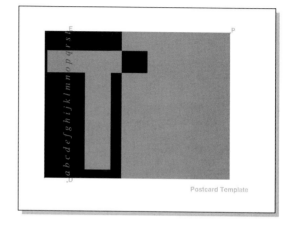

11 Choose Artwork & Template from the View menu.

12 Choose Save from the File menu.

Creating the "Type & design" overlay

1 Click the Type tool in the toolbox to create a new text object.

2 Position the pointer on point F, and click the mouse button.

3 Type the following, with a carriage return at the end of each line:

**TYPE
&
design**

4 Choose Select All from the Edit menu or press Control-A for the Select All command.

5 Choose Alignment from the Type menu and Centered from the submenu.

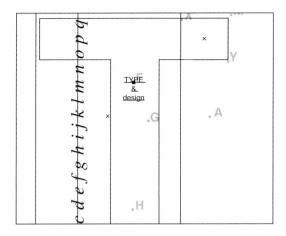

6 Choose Paint Style from the Paint menu.

7 Choose White under Fill, and click Apply.

8 Double-click the word *TYPE* to select it.

9 Press Control-T for the Type Style command and set the type attributes as follows:

Font: Helvetica-Bold
Size: 36 pt
Vert. Shift: -5
Horiz. Scale: 145
Spacing Options: Desired Letter Spacing: 0

Modifying the ampersand

1 Double-click the ampersand (&) to select it.

2 Set the type attributes as follows:

Font: Times-Bold
Size: 72 pt
Vert. Shift: 15
Horiz. Scale: 130

3 Choose Paint Style from the Paint menu.

4 Choose Black under Fill, type **80**, and click Apply.

Modifying the word design

1 Double-click to select the word *design*.

2 Set the type attributes as follows:

Font: Times-BoldItalic
Size: 48 pt
Vert. Shift: 20
Horiz. Scale: 100
Spacing Options: Desired Letter Spacing: 0

3 Choose Preview Illustration from the View menu.

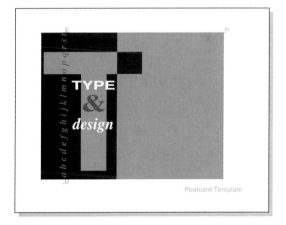

4 Choose Artwork & Template from the View menu.

5 Choose Save from the File menu.

Creating the curve for type on a path

1 Select the Centered-oval tool.

2 Move the pointer to point G, next to the ampersand (&), and click the mouse button.

TIP: CHOOSING SELECT
ALL WHEN THE INSER-
TION POINT IS WITH-
IN A TEXT OBJECT WILL
SELECT ALL OF THE
TEXT IN THE OBJECT.
CHOOSING SELECT ALL
WHEN THE POINTER
IS OUTSIDE A TEXT
OBJECT WILL SELECT
ALL THE ARTWORK
AND TEXT OBJECTS IN
THE DOCUMENT.

3 Type **291** for both Width and Height, and click OK.

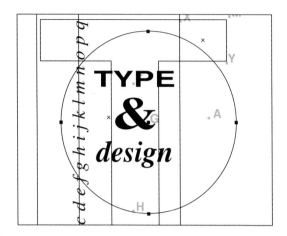

4 Choose the Direct-selection tool.

5 Click away from the artwork to deselect everything.

6 Click the edge of the circle to select it.

7 Click the leftmost anchor point of the circle.

8 Press the Backspace key to delete the left half of the circle.

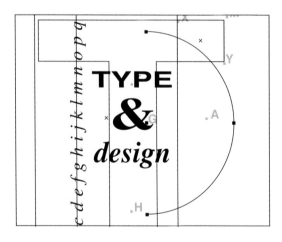

Creating text on the curve

1 Select the Type tool.

2 Position the pointer on the rightmost anchor point of the semicircle, and click the mouse button.

3 Type **competition** in lower-case letters.

4 Double-click to select the entire word.

5 Set the type attributes as follows:

Font: Helvetica
Size: 31
Vert. Shift: 0
Horiz. Scale: 140
Alignment: Centered
Spacing Options: Desired Letter Spacing: 145

6 Press Control-I for the Paint Style command and set the paint attributes as follows:

Fill: Process Color, M-45, Y-45, K-15

7 Choose Preview Illustration from the View menu.

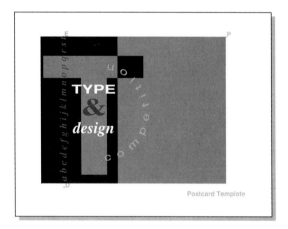

Postcard Template

8 Choose Artwork & Template from the View menu.

9 Choose Save from the File menu.

Creating the "1991" type

1 Using the Type tool, position the pointer on point H, and click the mouse button.

2 Type **1991**.

3 Double-click to select *1991*.

4 Choose Type Style from the Type menu.

5 Set the type attributes as follows:

Font: Times-Roman
Size: 36
Tracking: -50
Vert. Shift: 0
Horiz. Scale: 130
Spacing Options: Desired Letter Spacing: 0

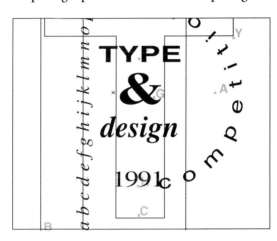

6 Click the Selection tool.

Note: When you click the Selection tool (or any tool) after creating type, the entire type object is selected.

7 With the type object selected, use the Right or Left Arrow keys to center *1991* inside the outline of the *T.*

8 Select the Type tool.

9 Drag to select the first *1* in *1991*.

10 Choose Type Style from the Type menu or press Control-T for the Type Style command, type **-40** for Vert. Shift in the Type Style dialog box, and click Apply.

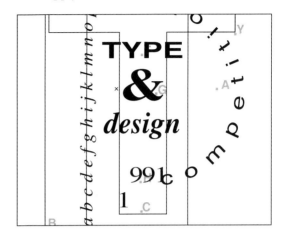

11 Drag to select the first *9* in *1991*.

12 Choose Type Style from the Type menu, type **-20** for Vert. Shift in the Type Style dialog box, and click Apply.

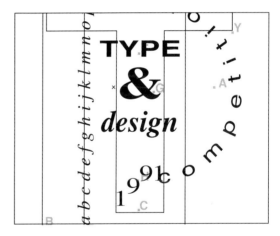

13 Drag to select the last *1* in *1991*.

14 Choose Type Style from the Type menu, type **20** for Vert. Shift in the Type Style dialog box, and click Apply.

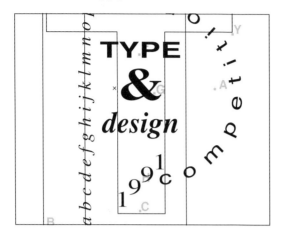

15 Double-click to select *1991*.

16 Set the paint attributes as follows:

Fill: Process Color, M-75, Y-75, K-20

17 Choose Preview Illustration from the View menu or press Control-Y for the Preview Illustration command.

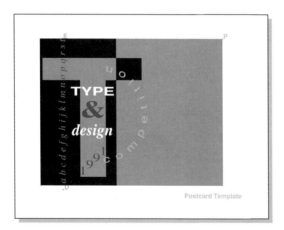

18 Choose Artwork & Template from the View menu.

19 Choose Save from the File menu.

Creating linked type objects

1 Select the Rectangle tool.

2 Position the pointer on point I (above and to the right of point M), and drag down and right to point K to create a rectangle.

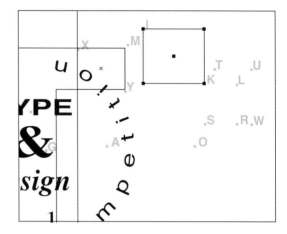

3 Choose the Selection tool.

4 Position the pointer on the top right anchor point of the rectangle, hold down the Alternate key, and drag to point L. Remember to release the mouse button before you release the Alternate key.

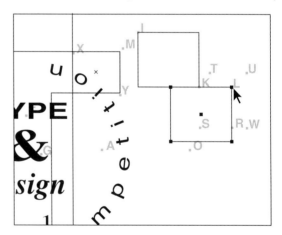

5 Choose Transform Again from the Arrange menu or press Control-D for the Transform Again command.

You should have three boxes.

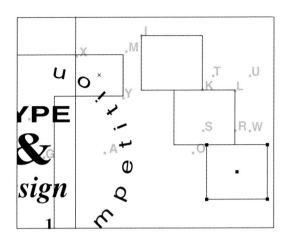

6 Select the Type tool.

7 Move the pointer to the left edge of the first box. The pointer should be an I-beam inside a dotted circle, and the Information Bar should read "Area Type."

Notice that the Information Bar and the type pointers change, depending on whether the pointer is on a path, a text object, or no existing artwork.

8 Click the mouse button. A blinking insertion point will appear.

9 Choose Import from the File menu and Text from the submenu.

10 Double-click the file called *POSTTXT.SAM*.

Type flows into the first rectangle.

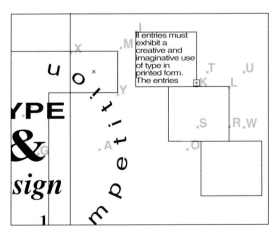

11 Choose Select All from the Edit menu.

12 Set the type attributes as follows:

Font: Helvetica
Size: 8.5 pt
Leading: 14 pt
Tracking: -25
Vert. Shift: 0
Alignment: Justified

When you have entered these values, click OK.

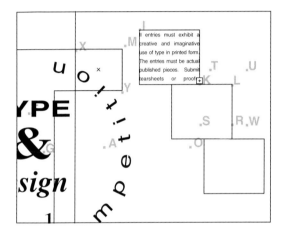

13 Choose the Selection tool.

14 Hold down the Shift key, and click the edge of the other two rectangles. All three rectangles should be selected.

15 Choose Link from the Type menu. The type flows into the other two rectangles.

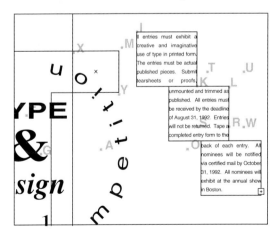

16 Choose Lock from the Arrange menu. This locks the three boxes so that they cannot be selected.

CREATING THE ENLARGED "A"

To create the large *A* at the beginning of the text object, you first create and paint the letter. Next you create a graphic boundary around the *A*. Finally, you make the text wrap around the graphic boundary.

Creating and painting the A

1 Select the Zoom-in tool.

2 Position the pointer on point M, and click the mouse button twice to zoom in.

3 Select the Type tool.

4 Position the pointer on point M, and click the mouse button.

5 Type a capital **A**.

6 Drag to select the *A*.

7 Choose Type Style from the Type menu or press Control-T for the Type Style command.

8 Set the type attributes as follows:

Font: Helvetica-Bold
Size: 65
Tracking: 0
Auto Leading: On
Alignment: Left

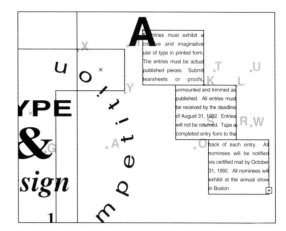

9 Press Control-I for the Paint Style command and set the paint attributes as follows:

Fill: Process Color, M-100, Y-100, K-40

10 Choose Preview Illustration from the View menu.

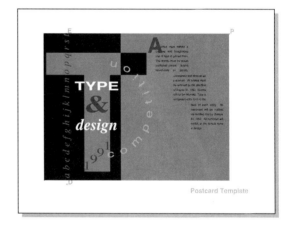

Postcard Template

11 Choose Artwork & Template from the View menu.

CREATING A GRAPHIC BOUNDARY

A graphic boundary is an unfilled, unstroked path around a graphic object (in this case, around the letter *A*). Creating a graphic boundary gives you more flexibility in adjusting the distances between the artwork and the text when you make the text wrap.

Creating the drop cap boundary

1 Choose the Centered-rectangle tool.

2 Position the pointer in the center of the *A*, and click the mouse button.

3 Type **48** for Width and **48** for Height, and click OK.

4 Use the arrow keys on the keyboard to center the rectangle around the *A*.

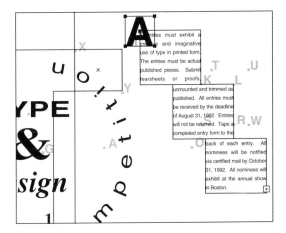

5 Choose Paint Style from the Paint menu.

6 Choose None under Fill and None under Stroke, and click OK.

Because the rectangle is unfilled and unstroked, you do not see it when you preview.

Modifying the drop cap boundary

1 Choose the Direct-selection tool.

2 Click away from the artwork to deselect it.

3 Click the upper right corner of the rectangle to select the anchor point.

4 Press the Left Arrow key until the right side of the rectangle is parallel to the right side of the *A*, as shown.

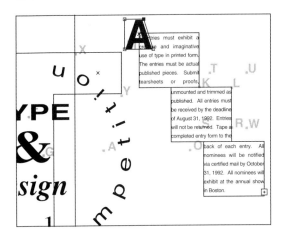

5 Choose the Selection tool.

6 Click away from the artwork to deselect it.

7 Choose Unlock All from the Arrange menu. The three linked text objects should be selected.

8 Hold down the Shift key, and click the edge of the shape around the *A*.

9 Choose Make Text Wrap from the Type menu.

10 Choose Preview Illustration from the View menu.

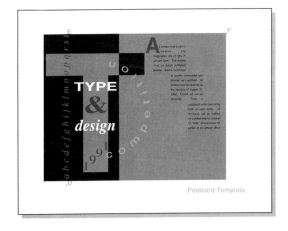

11 Choose Artwork & Template from the View menu.

12 Select the Zoom-out tool and click the *A*.

13 Choose Save from the File menu.

Creating a discretionary hyphen

1 Select the Type tool.

2 Click between the *g* and the *i* in *imaginative* (located in the first column).

3 Press Control-Shift-Keypad Hyphen to add a discretionary hyphen (imag-inative). Double-click the word *and* just before *imaginative*.

4 Press the Backspace key to delete the word *and*.

Notice that the discretionary hyphen in *imagina-tive* is removed.

5 Choose Undo Clear from the Edit menu or press Control-Z for the Undo command. The word *and* is added, and the hyphen reappears.

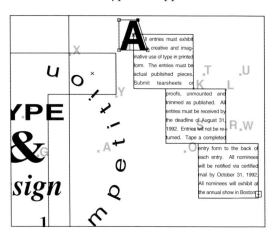

6 Choose Save from the File menu.

CREATING TYPE ON A PATH

In this part of the lesson, you create the *Call for Entries* text. First you create the path, and then you add the text.

Creating the path

1 Choose Actual Size from the View menu or press Control-H for the Actual Size command.

2 Select the Pen tool.

3 Click point N, located near the bottom right corner of the page.

4 Move the pointer to point O, above point N, hold down the Shift key, and click the mouse button.

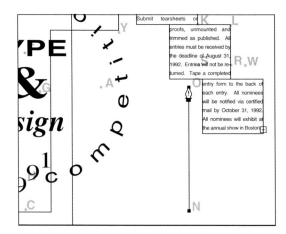

Adding type to the path

1 Select the Type tool.

2 Position the pointer on point N, and click the mouse button.

3 Type **Call for Entries**.

4 Choose Select All from the Edit menu.

5 Set the type attributes as follows:

Font: Helvetica-Bold
Size: 22
Tracking: 0
Horiz. Scale: 120
Auto Leading: On
Alignment: Left
Vert. Shift: 0

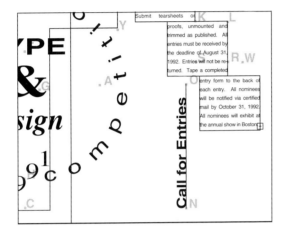

Creating a graphic object

1 Select the Rectangle tool.

2 Click near the top right of the screen.

3 Type **112** for Width and **184** for Height, and click OK.

4 Choose the Selection tool.

5 Position the pointer on the top right anchor point of the rectangle, and drag this anchor point to point P.

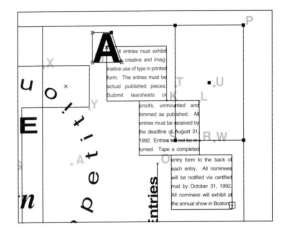

6 Select the Zoom-in tool.

7 Click point T once.

8 Select the Add-anchor-point tool.

9 Click point T to add an anchor point on the path.

10 Click on the rectangle near point W to add an anchor point on the path.

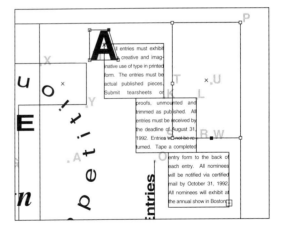

Modifying a graphic object

1 Choose the Direct-selection tool.

2 Position the pointer on the anchor point near point S, and drag to point U.

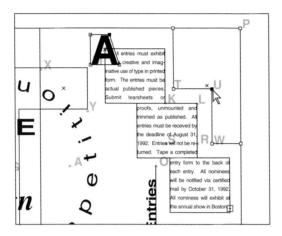

3 Choose Paint from the Style menu or press Control-I for the Paint Style command.

4 Choose Black under Fill, and click OK.

5 Choose Preview Illustration from the View menu.

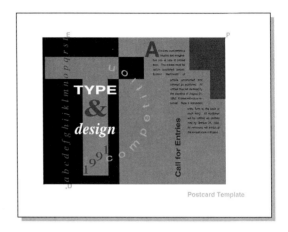

Postcard Template

6 Choose Save from the File menu.

7 Choose Print from the File menu.

8 Choose Close from the File menu.

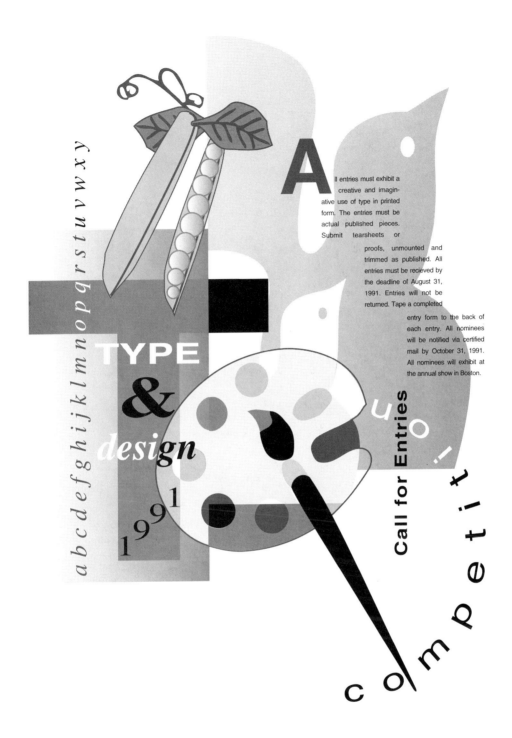

a b c d e f g h i j k l m n o p q r s t u v w x y

TYPE

&

design

1991

All entries must exhibit a creative and imaginative use of type in printed form. The entries must be actual published pieces. Submit tearsheets or proofs, unmounted and trimmed as published. All entries must be recieved by the deadline of August 31, 1991. Entries will not be returned. Tape a completed entry form to the back of each entry. All nominees will be notified via certified mail by October 31, 1991. All nominees will exhibit at the annual show in Boston.

Call for Entries

competition!

Lesson

6

LESSON 6: STAMP DESIGNS

This lesson is a directed study project designed to give you an opportunity to practice the techniques learned in lesson 1–3.

In this lesson you will create these stamps.

CREATING THE STAMP BASE

You will begin by creating the elements common to all four stamps: outside edge, background rectangle, and text. Using this base, you then add individual artwork to customize each stamp.

Creating the background

1 Choose Open from the File menu, and double-click *SGUIDE.AI.*

2 Take a moment to examine the file.

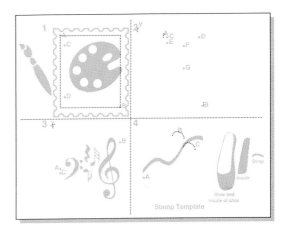

3 Choose Toolbox Options from the View menu and Reset Toolbox from the submenu.

4 Choose Preferences from the Edit menu.

5 Type **1** for Freehand Tolerance, and click OK.

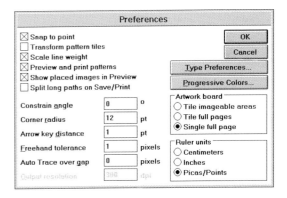

TIP: IF YOU NEED TO REPOSITION THE PAGE BOUNDARY, CHOOSE THE PAGE TOOL NEXT TO THE HAND TOOL. PRESS THE MOUSE AND MOVE THE RECTANGLE TO SURROUND THE PAGE. TO CHANGE ORIENTATION CHOOSE PRINT SETUP FROM THE FILE MENU, AND THEN CLICK LANDSCAPE AND OK.

6 Select the Auto Trace tool.

7 Position the pointer on the outside of the scalloped edge, and click the mouse button. (Make sure that you have not auto traced the letters *A* and *B* on the template. If you have traced these letters, delete the scalloped edge and auto trace it again.)

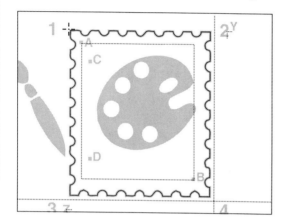

8 Set the paint attributes as follows:

Fill: White
Stroke: Black
Weight: .5

9 Select the Rectangle tool.

10 Position the pointer on the top left corner of the guide rectangle on point A.

11 Drag down and right to point B.

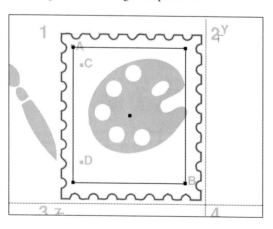

12 Set the paint attributes as follows:

Fill: Process Color, C-80, M-40, Y-0, K-0
Stroke: None

13 Choose Preview Illustration from the View menu.

14 Choose Artwork & Template from the View menu.

Creating the "29USA" text

1 Select the Zoom-in tool.

2 Click the top left corner of the rectangle.

3 Select the Type tool.

4 Position the pointer on point C, and click the mouse button.

5 Type **29USA**. (Make sure that *USA* is in capital letters.)

6 Drag to select the *29*.

7 Choose Type Style from the Type menu.

8 Set the type attributes as follows:

Font: Times-Bold
Size: 24
Horiz. Scale: 120

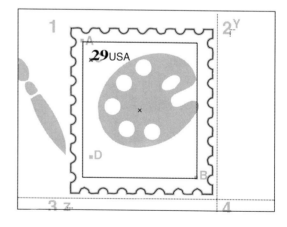

Be sure to click Apply when you have finished.

TIP: USE THE ALTERNATE KEY WHILE YOU DRAG ARTWORK TO MAKE A COPY. REMEMBER TO BEGIN DRAGGING, AND THEN HOLD DOWN THE ALTERNATE KEY. RE-LEASE THE MOUSE BUTTON BEFORE YOU RELEASE THE ALTER-NATE KEY. YOU CAN NOTE THE PROCESS IN THE STATUS LINE.

9 Drag to select *USA*.

10 Set the type attributes as follows:

Font: Times-Bold
Size: 12
Horiz. Scale: 100

Click OK.

11 With *USA* selected, hold down the Alternate and Shift keys, and press the Up Arrow key four times to vertically shift the selected text.

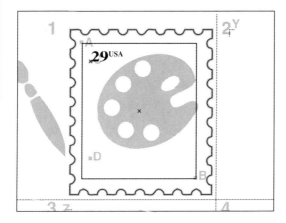

12 Click the Type tool. Notice that the text object becomes selected.

Creating the Support the Arts text

1 Position the pointer on point D at the bottom left corner of the stamp, and click the mouse button.

2 Type **Support** and press Return.

3 Type **the ARTS**.

4 Drag to select both lines of text.

5 Choose Type Style from the Type menu.

6 Set the type attributes as follows:

Font: Times Bold
Size: 18
Vert. Shift: 0
Alignment: Left

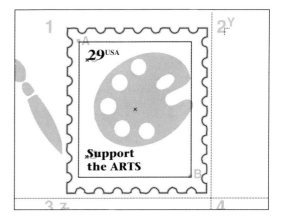

7 Select the Zoom-out tool, and click once to zoom out a level.

8 Choose the Selection tool.

9 Hold down the Shift key and click *29USA* to select both text objects.

10 Choose Paint Style from the Paint menu.

11 Choose White under Fill, and click OK.

12 Choose Save As from the File menu.

13 Type **STAMSTUD.AI**, and click OK.

Moving and copying the stamp base

Next you copy the base, so that you can use it for each of the four different stamps.

1 Select the Zoom-out tool, and click once.

2 Choose Select All from the Edit menu.

3 Choose Group from the Arrange menu or press Control-G for the Group command.

4 Choose the Selection tool.

5 Position the pointer on the top left corner of the scalloped edge, and begin dragging to the right.

6 Hold down the Alternate and Shift keys, and drag the artwork to corner guide Y. Release the mouse button before you release the Alternate and Shift keys. You now have two copies of the stamp base.

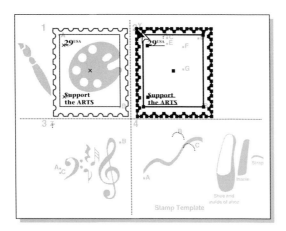

7 Choose Select All from the Edit menu.

8 Position the pointer on the top left corner of stamp 1, near point A, and begin dragging down. Hold down the Alternate and Shift keys, and continue to drag to corner guide Z. You now have four copies of the stamp base.

9 Choose Select All from the Edit menu.

10 Choose Lock from the Arrange menu or press Control-1 for the Lock command. When you lock artwork, you cannot select it. This allows you to

work on other parts of the file without changing the base art.

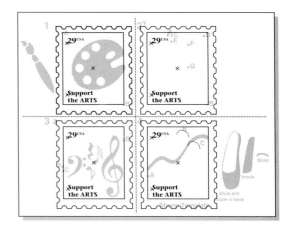

11 Choose Save from the File menu.

CREATING THE PALETTE STAMP

To create the artist's palette stamp, you will auto trace and paint the palette, and then auto trace and paint the paint brush. Finally, you will paint the background rectangle.

Creating the palette

1 Select the Zoom-in tool, and click once in the center of stamp 1.

2 Select the Auto Trace tool.

3 Position the pointer on the edge of the paint palette in stamp 1, and click the mouse button.

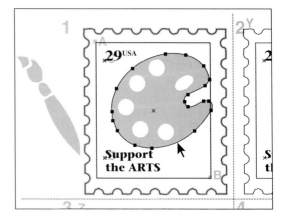

4 Set the paint attributes as follows:

Fill: White
Stroke: None

5 Position the pointer on the edge of the thumb hole, and click the mouse button.

6 Set the paint attributes as follows:

Fill: Process Color, C-80, M-40, Y-0, K-0

7 Use the Auto Trace tool to create each of the five paint spots.

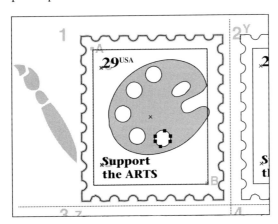

8 Choose the Selection tool.

9 Click the edge of the top paint spot.

10 Set the paint attributes as follows:

Fill: Process Color, C-0, M-50, Y-100, K-0
Stroke: None

Click Apply.

11 Working counterclockwise from the top, select and paint the remaining paint spots with the attributes below. Be sure to apply the attributes for each paint spot.

SECOND

Fill: Process Color, C-0, M-100, Y-0, K-0
Stroke: None
Click Apply.

THIRD

Fill: Process Color, C-0, M-0, Y-100, K-0
Stroke: None
Click Apply.

FOURTH

Fill: Process Color, C-100, M-0, Y-100, K-0
Stroke: None
Click Apply.

LAST

Fill: Process Color, C-100, M-100, Y-0, K-0
Stroke: None

Click OK to close the Paint Style dialog box.

Creating the paint brush

1 If necessary, scroll or press the Space bar to access the Hand tool command to see the paint brush.

2 Select the Auto Trace tool.

3 Click the edge of each part of the brush (tip, brush, metal brush holder, and handle) to auto trace each part.

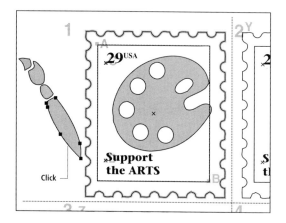

4 Choose the Selection tool.

5 Select each path and paint with these attributes:

TIP

> Fill: Process Color, C-0, M-100, Y-0, K-0
> Stroke: None

BRUSH

> Fill: Process Color, C-0, M-0, Y-0, K-100
> Stroke: None

METAL BRUSH HOLDER

> Fill: C-0, M-0, Y-0, K-20
> Stroke: None

HANDLE

> Fill: Process Color, C-0, M-0, Y-0, K-100
> Stroke, None

6 Choose the Object-selection tool.

7 Drag the pieces of the brush together to close up the spaces between the pieces.

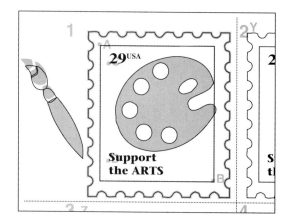

8 Hold down the Shift key, and click each piece until all four pieces are selected.

9 Choose Group from the Arrange menu.

10 Position the pointer on the bottom anchor point of the brush, and drag to point B.

11 Choose Preview Illustration from the View menu.

12 Choose Artwork & Template from the View menu.

13 Choose Save from the File menu.

CREATING THE FILM STAMP

You will use the Rectange and the Centered-rounded-rectangle tools to create the major elements of the film artwork. Once you have created the basic shapes, you will use the transform command to copy the shapes to get the true effect of film.

Creating the small rectangles on the film

1 Scroll until you see the stamp base for stamp 2.

2 Select the Rectangle tool.

3 Position the pointer on the guide line to the left of point A. Drag down and right to the corner guide at point B.

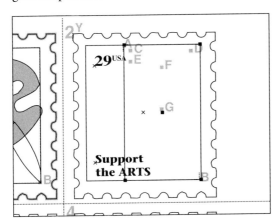

4 Set the paint attributes as follows:

Fill: Process Color, C-40, M-30, Y-0, K-10
Stroke: None

5 Select the Centered-rounded-rectangle tool.

6 Position the pointer on point C, and click the mouse button.

7 Type **10** for Width, **10** for Height, and **2** for Corner Radius, and click OK.

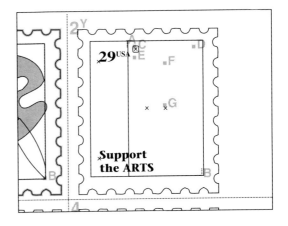

8 Set the paint attributes as follows:

Fill: Process Color, C-80, M-60, Y-0, K-20
Stroke: None

Copying the small rectangles

1 Choose the Object-selection tool.

2 Position the pointer on the center anchor point of the rectangle, and hold down the mouse button.

3 Hold down the Shift and Alternate keys, and drag to point D. Release the mouse button before you release the keys. You now have two rectangles.

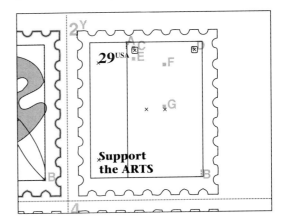

4 Hold down the Shift key, and click both rectangles to select them.

5 Choose Group from the Arrange menu.

6 Position the pointer on the center anchor point of the left rectangle.

7 Hold down the mouse button, and then hold down the Shift and Alternate keys.

8 Drag to point E. Release the mouse button before you release the keys. You now have four rectangles.

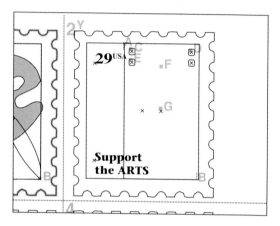

9 Choose Transform Again from the Arrange menu or press Control-D for the Transform Again command. Choose Transform Again until you have enough rectangles to reach the bottom of the background rectangle.

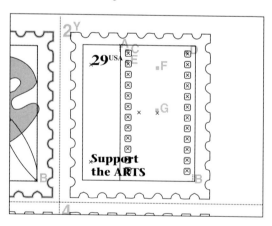

Creating the large rectangles on the film

1 Select the Centered-rounded-rectangle tool.

2 Position the pointer on point F, and click the mouse button.

3 Type **75** for Width, **63** for Height, and **4** for Corner Radius, and click OK.

4 Use the arrow keys to center the large rectangle between the left and right columns of smaller rectangles.

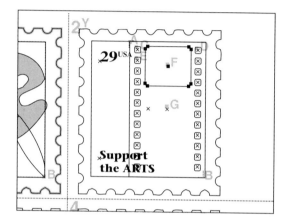

5 Choose the Selection tool.

6 Position the pointer on the center anchor point of the large rectangle. Hold down the mouse button, hold down the Alternate and Shift keys, and drag down to point G. Release the mouse button before you release the keys.

7 Choose Transform Again from the Arrange menu.

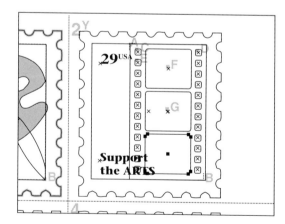

8 If necessary, use the Selection tool and the arrow keys to position the rectangles so they are equally spaced within the stamp.

9 Choose Preview Illustration from the View menu.

10 Choose Artwork & Template from the View menu or press Control-E for the Artwork & Template command.

Painting the background rectangle

1 Choose Unlock All from the Arrange menu.

2 Choose the Direct-selection tool.

3 Click away from the artwork to deselect everything.

4 Click the edge of the background rectangle.

5 Set the paint attributes as follows:

> **Fill: Process Color, C-80, M-60, Y-0, K-20**
> **Stroke: None**

6 Using the Direct-selection tool, click the baseline of the *29USA* text.

7 Hold down the Shift key and click the baseline of the *Support the ARTS* text.

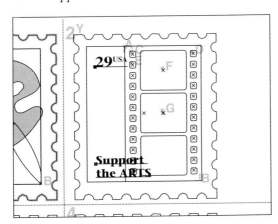

8 Choose Cut from the Edit menu. This copies the text to the pasteboard.

9 Choose Paste In Front from the Edit menu.

10 Choose Preview Illustration from the View menu.

11 Choose Artwork & Template from the View menu.

12 Choose Save from the File menu.

13 Select the Zoom-out tool, and click once.

CREATING THE MUSIC STAMP

You will use the Auto Trace tool to trace the shapes of the music notes for this stamp design. The Pen tool will be used to create one music bar. The Transform command will copy the music bar a number of times to create the music staff.

Creating the staff

1 Scroll until you see the stamp base for stamp 3.

2 Choose the Selection tool.

3 Click the scalloped border to select the grouped edge, rectangle, and text.

4 Choose Lock from the Arrange menu.

5 Select the Pen tool.

6 Position the pointer on point A, and click the mouse button.

7 Move the pointer to point B, and click the mouse button to draw a diagonal line.

8 Set the paint attributes as follows:

Fill: None
Stroke: White
Weight: 1

9 Choose the Object-selection tool.

10 Position the pointer on the anchor point at point A, and hold down the mouse button.

11 Hold down the Alternate and Shift keys, and drag to point C. Release the mouse button before you release the keys.

12 Choose Transform Again from the Arrange menu three times. There should be five parallel lines in the staff.

13 Select the Zoom-in tool, and click once.

Drawing the musical elements

1 Select the Auto Trace tool.

2 Click the edge of each musical element to auto trace it. After you have traced the *outside* of each element, auto trace the inner (hollow) portions. Use the Selection tool if you need to edit any anchor points.

3 Choose the Object-selection tool.

4 Hold down the Shift key, and click the musical elements until you have selected all of them. Be sure to include the hollow areas.

5 Set the paint attributes as follows:

Fill: Process Color, C-0, M-20, Y-75, K-0
Stroke: None

6 Using the Object-selection tool, click the top inner area of the clef.

7 Hold down the Shift key, and click the bottom inner area of the clef and both inner areas of the note.

8 Set the paint attributes as follows:

Fill: Process Color, C-80, M-60, Y-0, K-20
Stroke: None

9 Choose Bring To Front from the Edit menu.

10 Choose Preview Illustration from the View menu. Notice that the staff lines do not show in the hollow areas of the clef and the note.

Adding lines inside the clef and notes

1 Choose Artwork & Template from the View menu.

2 Select the Pen tool.

3 Click to draw short lines in the inner areas of the clef and the note. Remember to click the Pen tool after each path.

4 Choose the Selection tool.

5 Hold down the Shift key, and click to select all the lines you drew in the inner areas.

6 Set the paint attributes as follows:

Fill: None
Stroke: White
Weight: 1

7 Choose Preview Illustration from the View menu. Notice the white lines you just added.

8 Choose Artwork & Template from the View menu.

9 Choose Actual Size from the View Menu.

Painting the background rectangle

1 Choose Unlock All from the Arrange menu.

2 Choose the Direct-selection tool.

3 Click away from the artwork to deselect everything.

4 Click the edge of the background rectangle.

5 Set the paint attributes as follows:

Fill: Process Color, C-80, M-60,Y-0, K-20
Stroke: None

6 Choose Preview Illustration from the View menu.

7 Choose Artwork & Template from the View menu.

8 Choose Save from the File menu.

CREATING THE DANCE STAMP

For creating the artwork in the dance stamp you will first create the ribbon behind the ballet shoe. Next you will auto trace the shapes that make up the shoe. The last task you will do is move the pieces of the shoe to the appropriate location.

Creating the streamers

1 Scroll until you see the stamp base for stamp 4.

2 Choose the Selection tool.

3 Click the scalloped border to select the grouped edge, rectangle, and text.

4 Choose Lock from the Arrange menu.

5 Select the Auto Trace tool.

6 Click the edge of the streamer.

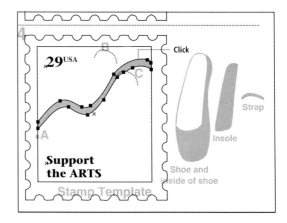

7 Choose the Object-selection tool.

8 Position the pointer on the top left anchor point, and hold down the mouse button.

9 Hold down the Shift and Alternate keys, and drag down to point A. Release the mouse button before you release the keys.

10 Choose Transform Again from the Arrange menu to create a third streamer.

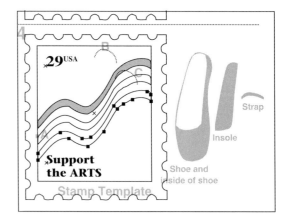

11 Using the Object-selection tool, hold down the Shift key, and click all three streamers to select them.

12 Set the paint attributes as follows:

Fill: White
Stroke: None

13 If necessary, use the arrow keys to fine-tune the position of the streamers inside the rectangle.

14 Click away from the artwork to deselect everything.

15 Choose Preview Illustration from the View menu.

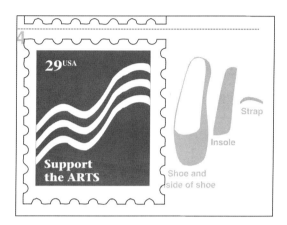

16 Choose Artwork & Template from the View menu.

Auto tracing the shoes

1 Scroll until you see the parts of the shoes on the template in the window.

2 Select the Auto Trace tool.

3 Auto trace the parts of the shoe in the following order: (1) outside of shoe, (2) inside of shoe, (3) insole, and (4) strap.

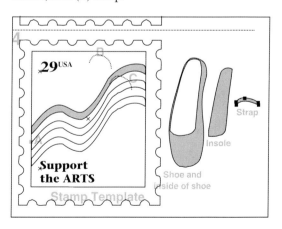

Drawing the shoes in this order assures that they will be properly layered when you move the pieces on top of one another.

Painting the pieces of the shoe

1 Choose the Object-selection tool.

2 Click the outside of the shoe.

3 Hold down the Shift key, and click the strap.

4 Set the paint attributes as follows:

Fill: Process Color, C-0, M-40, Y-0, K-0
Stroke: None

5 Click the inside of the shoe.

6 Set the paint attributes as follows:

Fill: White

7 Click to select the insole.

8 Set the paint attributes as follows:

Fill: Black, 10

9 Hold down the Shift key, and drag the insole into the shoe.

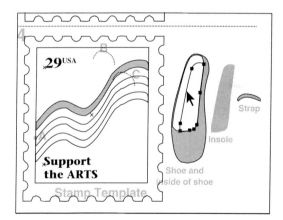

10 Select the strap, hold down the Shift key, and drag the strap into the shoe.

11 Choose Preview Illustration from the View menu.

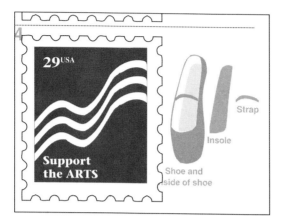

Check the layering order. If you need to change the layering order, switch to Artwork Only mode, and use the Send To Back or Bring To Front commands to relayer the shoe.

Grouping and moving the shoe

1 Drag a selection marquee around the entire shoe.

2 Choose Group from the Arrange menu.

3 Choose Artwork & Template from the View menu.

4 Drag until the heel of the shoe is on guide corner B. Then release the mouse button.

5 Drag the shoe by the heel down and right toward guide corner C. Hold down the Alternate key before you release the mouse button to make a copy of the shoe.

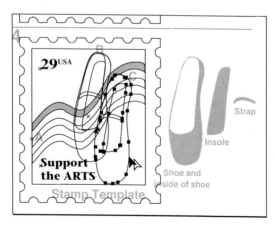

Painting the background rectangle

1 Choose Unlock All from the Arrange menu.

2 Choose the Direct-selection tool.

3 Click away from the artwork to deselect everything.

4 Click the edge of the background rectangle.

5 Set the paint attributes as follows:

> **Fill: Process Color, C-80, M-40, Y-0, K-0Stroke: None**

6 Using the Direct-selection tool, click the baseline of the *29USA* text.

7 Hold down the Shift key, and click the baseline of the *Support the ARTS* text.

8 Choose Cut from the Edit menu. This copies the text to the pasteboard.

9 Choose Paste In Front from the Edit menu.

10 Choose Preview Illustration from the View menu.

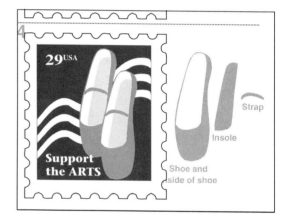

11 Choose Artwork & Template from the View menu.

12 Choose Save from the File menu.

13 Choose Print from the File menu.

14 Choose Close from the File menu.

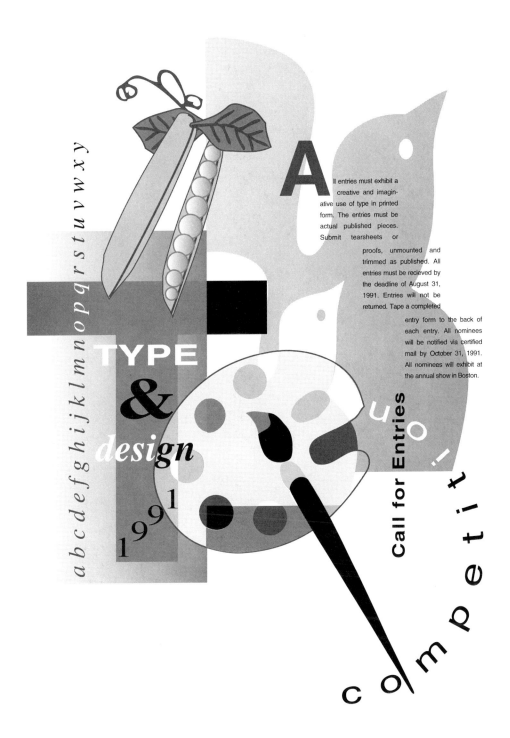

TYPE

&

design

1991

a b c d e f g h i j k l m n o p q r s t u v v w x y

All entries must exhibit a creative and imaginative use of type in printed form. The entries must be actual published pieces. Submit tearsheets or proofs, unmounted and trimmed as published. All entries must be recieved by the deadline of August 31, 1991. Entries will not be returned. Tape a completed entry form to the back of each entry. All nominees will be notified via certified mail by October 31, 1991. All nominees will exhibit at the annual show in Boston.

Call for Entries

competition!

Lesson

7

LESSON 7: USING THE TRANSFORMATION TOOLS

You can transform any number of objects from a single anchor point to all of the objects in a document. The transformation tools let you modify the physical shape, size, and appearance of objects. You can transform objects using transformation tools alone or in a sequence.

SCALING

The scale tools allow you to change the horizontal and vertical proportions of all selected points and paths. These proportions can be adjusted uniformly or nonuniformly, and the percentage of scale can be specified either visually or numerically.

Scaling is always to a base point, called the *origin*. This point determines the center of the scaling action, that is, the point around which the scaling will take place.

Visually scaling a selection

1 Choose Open from the File menu, and double-click the file named *CARROT.AI*.

2 Choose Toolbox Options from the View menu, and Reset Toolbox from the submenu, or hold down the Shift key and double-click any tool in the toolbox to reset the toolbox.

3 Choose Print Setup from the File menu, and click Portrait and OK.

4 Select the Hand tool, and move the page so that the top carrot is centered on the left side of your screen.

5 Choose Preview Illustration from the View menu.

6 Choose the Selection tool, and click to select the carrot.

7 Select the Scale tool. The pointer will change to a dotted +. Position the pointer on the tip of the carrot, and click the mouse button. This establishes the origin for scaling. After you click, the pointer changes to an arrowhead.

Watch the Status Line for Scale tool tips.

8 Position the pointer just above and to the right of the carrot.

9 Begin dragging up and to the right; then hold down the Shift key to scale the object proportionally.

10 Hold down the Alternate key to make a copy of the new, scaled carrot.

11 Release the mouse button, and then release the keys.

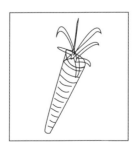

TIP: HOLDING DOWN THE
SHIFT KEY WHILE YOU
ROTATE CONSTRAINS
THE ROTATION TO
45-DEGREE ANGLES.

Numerically scaling a selection

You can use the Scale-dialog tool to specify an exact rate of horizontal and vertical scaling of a selection by supplying a numerical percentage.

1 Scroll down until the bottom carrot is in the middle of the screen.

2 Choose the Selection tool, and click to select the carrot.

3 Select the Scale-dialog tool. The pointer changes to a + with a tail.

4 Position the pointer at the bottom of the carrot, and click the mouse button. The Scale dialog box appears.

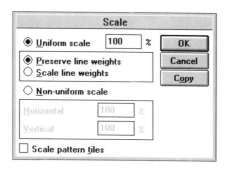

5 Click Uniform Scale, and type 500. This will create a new object that is five times (500%) as big as the selection.

6 Click OK to scale the carrot.

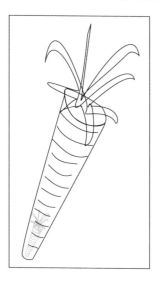

7 Position the pointer at the bottom of the carrot, and click the mouse button.

8 Type 50, and click OK. The new carrot is one-half (50%) the size of the last carrot.

9 Choose Close from the File menu. Do not save changes.

ROTATING

The rotate tools allow you to rotate all selected points and paths around a specified pivot point. The degree of rotation can be specified either visually or numerically.

Rotating with the rotate tools is always relative to a pivot point called the *origin*. This point determines the center of rotation, that is, the point around which the selection will spin.

Visually rotating a selection

1 Choose Open from the File menu, or press Control-O for the Open command, and double-click the file named *HARP.AI*.

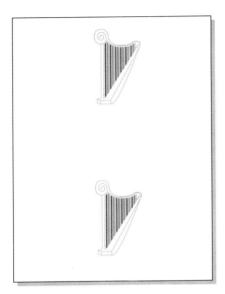

2 Scroll to position the artwork so that the top harp is centered on your screen.

3 Choose Preview Illustration from the View menu.

4 Choose the Selection tool, and click to select the harp.

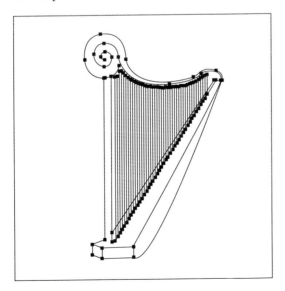

5 Select the Rotate tool. The pointer changes to a dotted +.

6 Position the pointer at the bottom-left corner of the harp, and click the mouse button. This establishes the origin around which the harp will revolve. After you click, the pointer changes to an arrowhead.

7 Move the pointer near the top-right corner of the harp. Hold down the mouse button and drag down and right to rotate the object. (If you hold down the Shift key while you drag, the rotation is constrained to 45-degree angles around the origin.)

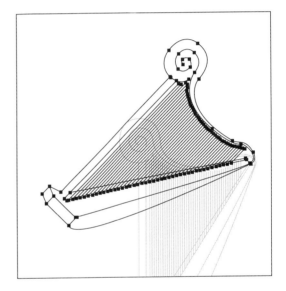

8 Hold down the Alternate key before you release the mouse button to make a copy at the new, rotated angle.

9 Choose Transform Again from the Arrange menu, or press Control-D for the Transform Again command, to repeat the copied rotation and create additional copies.

Numerically rotating a selection

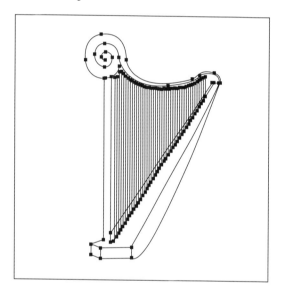The Rotate-dialog tool allows you to express the exact amount of rotation for all selected points and paths by specifying the amount of rotation in degrees. The degree of rotation can be expressed in positive or negative values; a negative value rotates the selection clockwise, and a positive value rotates the selection counterclockwise.

1 Scroll down until the bottom harp is in the middle of the screen.

2 Choose the Selection tool, and click to select the bottom harp.

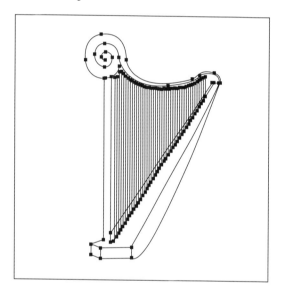

3 Select the Rotate-dialog tool. The pointer changes to a dotted + with a tail.

4 Position the pointer at the bottom-left corner of the harp, and click the mouse button. The Rotate dialog box appears.

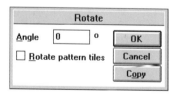

5 Type -45 after Angle to rotate the object 45 degrees clockwise.

6 Click Copy to create a rotated duplicate of the object.

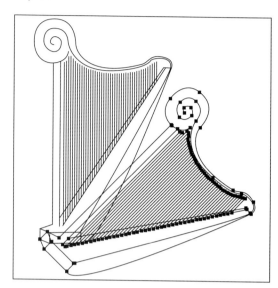

7 Close the file. Do not save changes.

REFLECTING

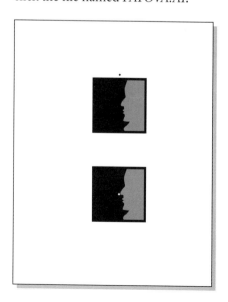The reflect tools allow you to mirror all selected points and paths across a specified axis of reflection. Mirroring with the reflect tools is always relative to the *axis of reflection*. This axis determines the line across which the selection will be reflected.

Reflecting a selection

1 Choose Open from the File menu, and double-click the file named *FATOVA.AI*.

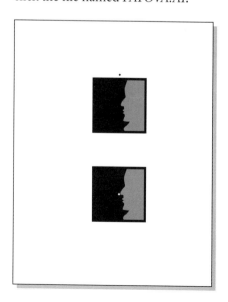

2 Scroll to position the page so the artwork is centered on your screen.

3 Choose Preview Illustration from the View menu.

4 Choose the Selection tool.

5 Click to select the shape inside the top rectangle. Do not select the rectangle.

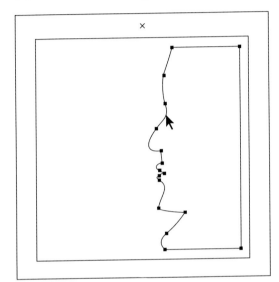

6 Select the Reflect tool.

7 Position the pointer in the center of the rectangle, and click the mouse button. This establishes one of the points of the imaginary line across which the path will reflect.

8 Hold down the Shift key. This constrains the imaginary line to vertical.

9 Hold down the Alternate key. This will create a copy of the reflected object.

10 Position the pointer outside the top of the rectangle, directly above the center.

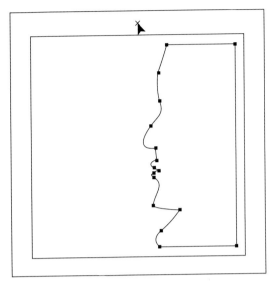

11 Click the mouse button. Then release the keys. The point where you click defines the second point of the imaginary line.

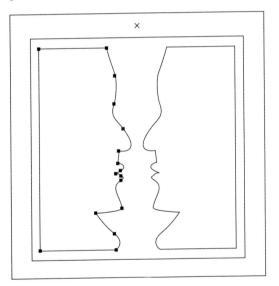

12 Choose Close from the File menu. Do not save changes.

SHEARING

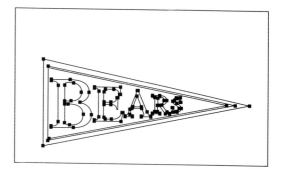 The shear tools allow you to slant all selected points and paths at a specified angle. The angle of shear can be specified visually, or it can be locked to the horizontal or vertical or to a specified angle with the Shear-dialog tool. Slanting with the Shear tool is always done along an *angle of shear*, which is defined by two points.

Shearing a selection

1 Choose Open from the File menu, and double-click the file named *PENNANT.AI* to open it.

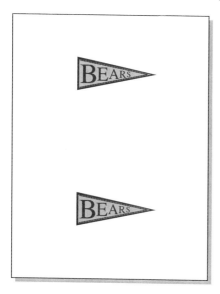

2 Position the artwork so that the top pennant is in the center of the screen.

To get the dialog box with the regular Shear tool, hold down the Alternate key and click the mouse button.

3 Choose Preview Illustration from the View menu.

4 Choose the Selection tool, and click to select the pennant. (The pennant has been grouped so you can shear it as a single object.)

5 Select the Shear tool. The pointer changes to a dotted +.

6 Position the pointer near the bottom-left corner of the pennant, and click the mouse button. This establishes one of the points that determine the angle at which the path will slant. After you click, the pointer changes to an arrowhead.

7 Move the pointer to the right side of the pennant. Hold down the mouse button and drag slowly to the right to stretch the pennant.

8 Still holding down the mouse button, drag upward to stretch the pennant in a different direction.

You can also shear objects numerically by using the Shear-dialog tool.

9 Choose Close from the File menu. Do not save changes.

TIP: THE BLEND TOOL CAN BE USED ON EITHER TWO CLOSED PATHS OR TWO OPEN PATHS. YOU CANNOT BLEND FROM AN OPEN PATH TO A CLOSED PATH. WHEN BLENDING BE- TWEEN TWO OPEN PATHS, YOU MUST BLEND FROM THE END- POINTS OF EACH PATH.

BLENDING

The Blend tool allows you to blend shapes, colors, and line thicknesses from one path to another. Some of the effects that can be achieved with the Blend tool include radial and straight gra- dations, irregular gradations, shading on objects, and various kinds of shape interpolations.

Blending shapes and line weights

1 Choose Open from the File menu, and double- click the file named *BLENDART.AI* to open it.

2 Scroll to position the artwork for the hand and the foot in the middle of the screen.

3 Choose Preview Illustration from the View menu. Notice the different line weights of the hand and the foot.

4 Choose the Selection tool, and drag a marquee around both the hand and the foot so that all points on both objects are selected.

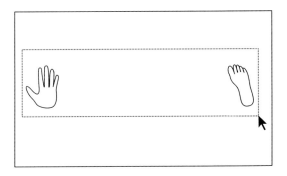

5 Select the Blend tool.

6 Click the bottom anchor point on the hand.

7 Move the pointer to the foot, and click the bottom-right anchor point. The Blend dialog box appears.

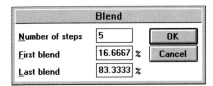

8 Type 5 for Number of Steps, and click OK.

9 Choose the Selection tool, and click away from the artwork to deselect everything.

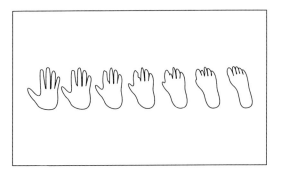

Blending colors and shapes

You can use the Blend tool to blend colors as well as shapes.

1 Select the Zoom-out tool, and click once in the center of the page.

2 Scroll until the stars artwork is in the middle of the screen.

3 Use the Selection tool to drag a marquee around the large star to select all points on both objects.

4 Select the Blend tool.

5 Click the top anchor point of the large star.

6 Click the top-left anchor point of the small star. The figure below shows which points you should have clicked.

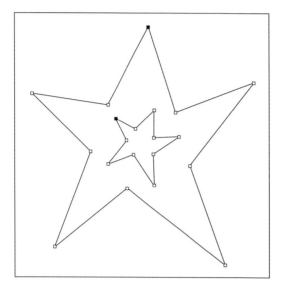

7 Type 24 for Number of Steps, and click OK.

8 Choose Artwork Only from the View menu, or press Control-W for the Artwork Only command, to see the artwork.

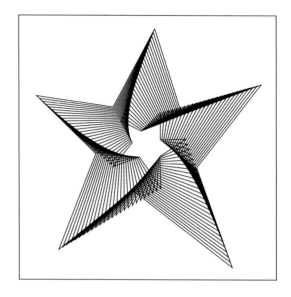

9 Close all files. Do not save changes.

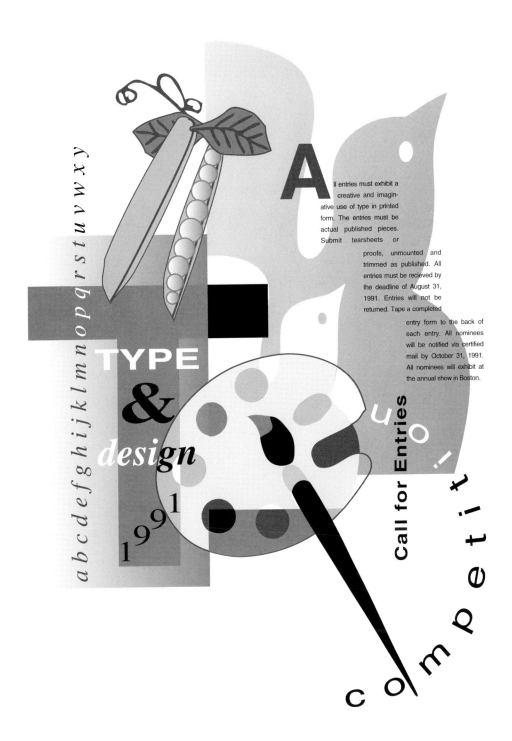

a b c d e f g h i j k l m n o p q r s t u v w x y

All entries must exhibit a creative and imaginative use of type in printed form. The entries must be actual published pieces. Submit tearsheets or proofs, unmounted and trimmed as published. All entries must be recieved by the deadline of August 31, 1991. Entries will not be returned. Tape a completed entry form to the back of each entry. All nominees will be notified via certified mail by October 31, 1991. All nominees will exhibit at the annual show in Boston.

TYPE

&

design

1991

Call for Entries

competition

Lesson

8

LESSON 8: CREATING PATTERNS

P atterns are an arrangement of objects into a regular, repeating design. You can create patterns from scratch with any of the tools in the Adobe Illustrator program.

CREATING A PATTERN

You create a pattern by drawing a bounding rectangle in back of the artwork. The bounding rectangle defines the *pattern tile*. The pattern tile is the area that is repeated when you paint with a pattern.

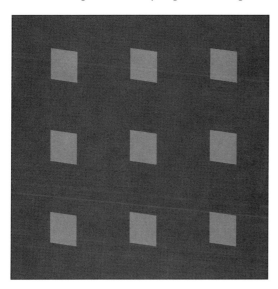

Creating the bounding rectangle

1 Choose New from the File menu or press Control-N to open a new file with no template.

2 Choose Preferences from the Edit menu, and click Inches under Ruler Units. Click OK.

3 Select the Centered-rectangle tool, and click in the center of the window.

4 Type **1.5** for Width, **1.5** for Height, and **0** for Corner Radius, and click OK.

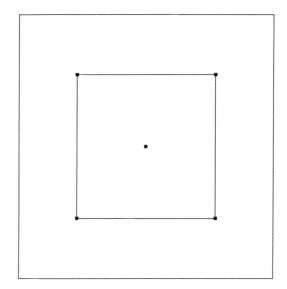

5 Choose Paint Style from the Paint menu. Choose Process Color under Fill. Type **100** for Cyan, **50** for Magenta, **0** for Yellow, and **20** for Black. Choose None under Stroke, and click OK.

Drawing and painting the pattern artwork

1 Using the Centered-rectangle tool, click the top-left corner of the original rectangle.

2 Type **.5** for Height and **.5** for Width, and click OK.

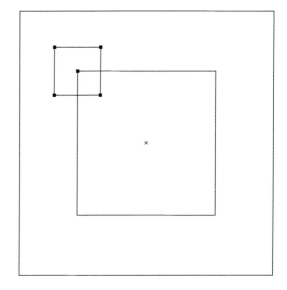

TIP: HOLDING DOWN
THE ALTERNATE KEY
WHILE YOU DRAG
CREATES A COPY OF
THE SELECTED OBJECT.
BE SURE TO RELEASE
THE MOUSE BUTTON
BEFORE YOU RELEASE
THE ALTERNATE KEY.

3 Choose Paint Style from the Paint menu. Under Fill, choose Process Color. Type **80** for Cyan, **30** for Magenta, and **10** for Black. Click OK.

Adjusting the shape of the square

1 Choose the Direct-selection tool.

2 Click away from the artwork to deselect everything.

3 Click the top-right corner of the small square.

4 Use the Up Arrow key on the keyboard, and press it five times to move the segment up.

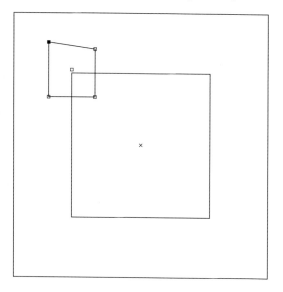

5 Click the bottom-left corner of the small square.

6 Use the Down Arrow key on the keyboard, and press it five times to move the segment down to create a diamond shape.

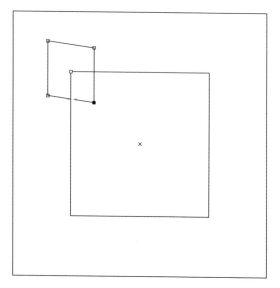

Moving and copying the diamond

1 Choose the Selection tool, and click the diamond.

2 Position the pointer on the center anchor point of the diamond, and drag it to the top-right anchor point of the large square. The pointer turns hollow to show it is snapped to point.

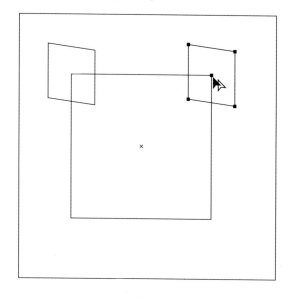

3 Hold down the Alternate key and release the mouse button to make a copy.

4 Hold down the Shift key and click the leftmost diamond to select both diamonds.

5 Position the pointer on the center anchor point of the left diamond, and drag both diamonds down until the pointer snaps to the anchor point on the bottom-left corner of the square.

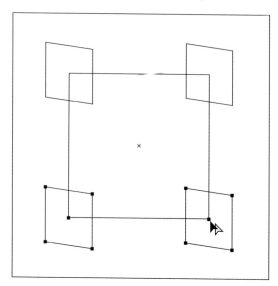

6 Hold down the Alternate key and release the mouse button first.

7 Position the pointer on the center anchor point of the top-left diamond, and drag it to the center anchor point of the large square.

8 Hold down the Alternate key and release the mouse button first.

Defining a pattern

1 Use the Selection tool, and drag a marquee to select the diamonds and square.

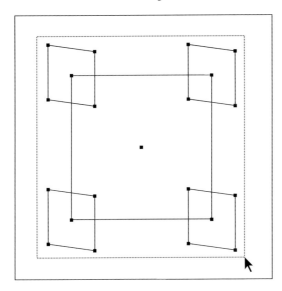

2 Choose Pattern from the Paint menu. Click New.

The pattern is previewed in the lower-right corner of the dialog box.

3 Type **Diamonds** for Pattern Name, and click OK.

4 Choose Select All from the Edit menu.

5 Press the Delete or Backspace key to delete the artwork.

Painting with a pattern

1 Choose the Centered-rectangle tool, and click in the center of the screen.

2 Type **5** for Width and **5** for Height, and click OK.

3 Choose Paint Style from the Paint menu, or press Control-I for the Paint Style command, and choose Pattern under Fill. Click *Diamonds,* and click OK.

4 Choose Preview Illustration from the View menu to see the pattern-filled rectangle.

5 Choose Artwork Only from the View Menu, or press Control-W for the Artwork Only command.

Transferring a pattern to the Adobe Illustrator startup file

1 Choose the Selection tool, and click the rectangle that you filled with the diamond pattern.

2 Choose the Scale dialog tool, and click in the center of the rectangle. Type **25** for Uniform scale. Click the Scale Pattern tiles option, and click OK.

3 Choose Copy from the Edit menu, or press Control-C for the Copy command.

4 Choose Open from the File menu, click the file named *STARTUP.AI*, and click OK.

5 Choose Paste from the Edit menu, or press Control-V for the Paste command to paste the pattern-filled rectangle in the *STARTUP.AI* file.

6 With the Selection tool, position the rectangle in a new location.

7 Choose Save from the File menu, or press Control-S for the Save command, and click OK to replace the *STARTUP.AI* file.

8 Choose Close from the File menu to close the Startup file.

9 Choose Close from the File menu to close the file that you used to create the pattern. Do not save changes.

Note: *The STARTUP.AI file must be kept in the directory named AI4.*

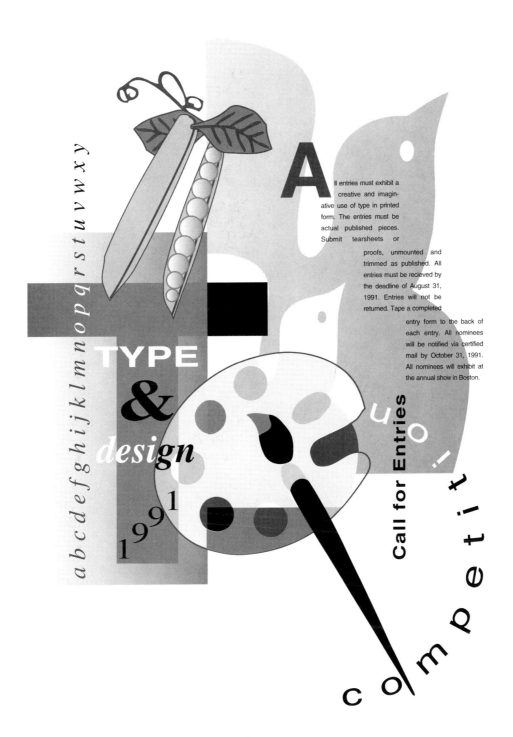

a b c d e f g h i j k l m n o p q r s t u v v w x y

TYPE

&

design

1 9 9 1

A

ll entries must exhibit a creative and imagin- ative use of type in printed form. The entries must be actual published pieces. Submit tearsheets or

proofs, unmounted and trimmed as published. All entries must be recieved by the deadline of August 31, 1991. Entries will not be returned. Tape a completed

entry form to the back of each entry. All nominees will be notified via certified mail by October 31, 1991. All nominees will exhibit at the annual show in Boston.

Call for Entries

competition!

Lesson

9

LESSON 9: CREATING GRAPHS

You create a graph by drawing a basic outline of the graph with one of the graph tools and then entering data. You can enter data for graphs manually, or you can import data from other programs. You can customize graphs using colors and designs, and you can edit and enhance graphs using the transformation tools.

Adjusting the page orientation

1 Choose New from the File menu.

2 Choose Toolbox Options from the View menu and Reset Toolbox from the submenu.

3 Choose Print Setup from the File menu.

4 Click the Landscape icon, and click OK.

Creating a graph and entering data

1 Select the Grouped-column-graph tool.

2 Position the pointer in the upper-left corner of the window, and drag a rectangle approximately 4 inches by 5 inches. The Graph Data dialog box appears.

3 Type **Pears**, and press Enter.

4 Type **Grapes**, and press Enter.

5 Type **Cherries**.

6 Position the pointer in the cell next to Pears, and click the mouse button.

7 Type **3100**, and press Enter.

8 Type **2200**, and press Enter.

9 Type **1900**.

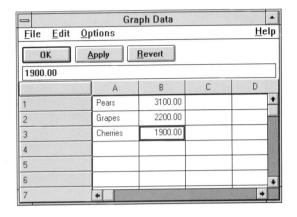

10 Click OK.

11 Choose Preview Illustration from the View menu, or press Control-Y for the Preview Illustration command.

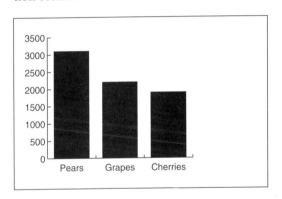

Transforming the graph

1 Choose Graph Data from the Graph menu, or press Control-Alternate-Shift-D for the Graph command.

2 In the Graph Data dialog box, choose Transpose from the Edit menu in the Graph data dialog box, and click OK.

3 Choose the Direct-up-selection tool, and click away from the graph to deselect everything.

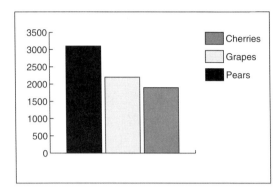

4 Choose Artwork Only from the View menu.

Painting a graph

1 Be sure that you have chosen the Direct-up-selection tool.

Note: Always keep in mind that graphs are grouped objects. As long as you want to change the values for the data, you must not ungroup the graph.

2 Click the edge of the legend box next to *Pears*. The legend box is selected. (Notice that the Status Line reads "Direct up selection," and a plus sign is added to the pointer.)

3 Click the edge of the legend box again. The column for Pears is now added to the selection.

4 Choose Paint Style from the Paint menu, or press Control-I for the Paint Style command.

5 Choose Custom Color under Fill, choose the color Pear, and click OK.

6 Choose Preview Illustration from the View menu.

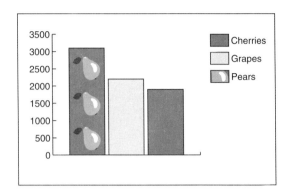

7 Choose Artwork Only from the View menu.

8 Choose the Selection tool, and click away from the graph to deselect everything.

9 Click the graph to select all of it. When you use the Selection tool, you select the entire graph, because it is grouped.

10 Choose Graph Data from the Graph menu, or press Control-Alternate-Shift-D for the Graph Data command.

11 Click 3100 under Pears, type **3300**, and click OK.

Creating and painting a pie graph

1 Choose Graph Style from the Graph menu or press Control-Alternate-Shift-S for the Graph Style command.

2 Click Pie under Graph type, and click Drop Shadow.

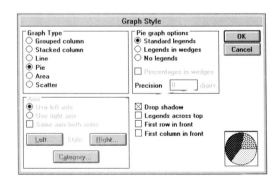

3 Click OK.

4 Choose Preview Illustration from the View Menu.

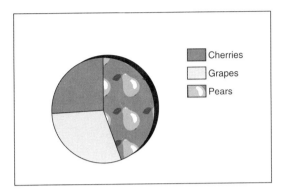

5 Choose the Direct-up-selection tool, and click away from the graph to deselect it.

6 Double-click the edge of the legend box next to *Cherries*. This direct-up-selects both the legend box and the pie wedge.

7 Choose Paint Style from the Paint menu; then move the Paint Style dialog box below your graph.

8 Choose Custom Color under Fill, choose the color Cherry, and click Apply.

9 Click away from the artwork to deselect everything.

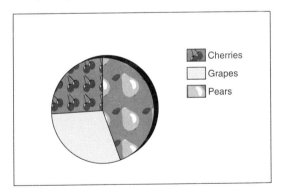

10 Double-click the edge of the legend box next to *Pears* so that the legend box and the column are selected.

11 Choose Paint Style from the Paint menu.

12 Choose Pattern under Fill, choose the Pear pattern, and click Apply.

13 Repeat steps 10 through 12 to select the Cherries legend box and column and fill them with the Cherries pattern. Then repeat the process for the Grapes.

14 Click away from the artwork to deselect everything.

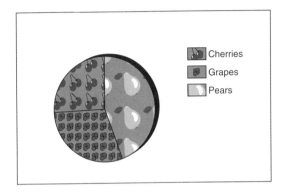

15 Choose Artwork Only from the View Menu.

Revising data

You can cut and paste data in the Graph Data window. You will add a column for the year 1993.

1 Choose the Selection tool, and click the graph to select it.

2 Choose Graph Data from the Graph menu.

3 Position the pointer in the top-left cell, and drag down and right to select all of the data.

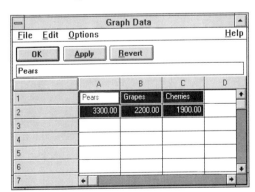

TIP: MOVE THE TYPE
STYLE DIALOG BOX SO
YOU CAN SEE THE TYPE
ON THE PAGE.

4 From the Graph Data dialog box, choose Cut from the Edit menu, or press Shift-Delete for the Cut command. The data is copied to the pasteboard.

5 Move the pointer to the top cell in the second column, and click the mouse button.

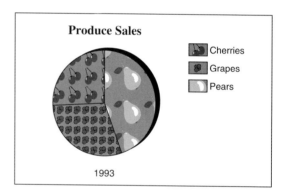

6 From the Graph Data dialog box, choose Paste from the Edit menu.

7 Move the pointer to the second box down in the first column (next to *3300*), and click the mouse button.

8 Type the following (including the quotation marks):

"**1993**"

9 Click OK.

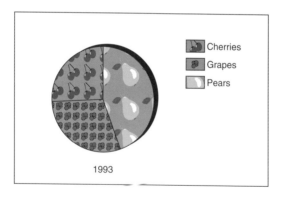

Adding type and setting type attributes

1 Select the Type tool, and click above the pie graph.

2 Type **Produce Sales.**

3 Click the Type tool in the toolbox to select the text object.

4 Choose Type Style from the Type menu or press Control-T for the Type Style command, and set the type attributes as described below. Be sure to apply the attributes.

> Font: Times-Bold
> Size: 30
> Alignment: Centered

5 Choose Paint Style from the Paint menu.

6 Choose Black for Fill, choose None for Stroke, and click OK.

Produce Sales

Cherries
Grapes
Pears

1993

7 Choose the Direct-up-selection tool, and click away from the artwork to deselect it.

8 Double-click the baseline of the word *Pears* to select all the elements from the same group (all of the legend names).

9 Choose Type Style from the Type menu.

10 Change the font to Times-Bold.

11 Type **15** for Size.

12 Click Apply.

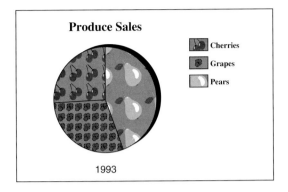

13 Click the baseline of the string *1993*.

14 Click on the Type Style dialog box.

15 Change the font to Times-Bold.

16 Type **30** for Size.

17 Click OK.

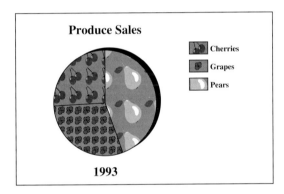

Creating an exploded pie graph

1 Use the Direct-up-selection tool, and drag a small selection marquee through the outer edge of the largest pie wedge.

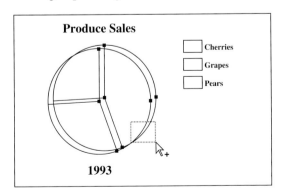

2 Press the Right and Up Arrow keys on the keyboard to move the selected wedge with its shadow away from the rest of the pie.

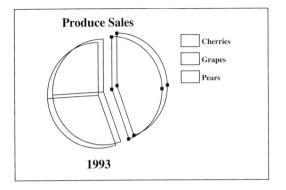

3 Choose Preview Illustration from the View menu.

4 Choose Artwork Only from the View menu.

5 Choose Save As from the File menu.

6 Type **PSALESG.AI**.

7 Click OK.

8 Choose Print from the File menu.

9 Choose Close from the File menu.

CUSTOMIZING A GRAPH

Once you have created a graph, you can customize it in innumerable ways. You can change the colors of shading in a graph, the type face, and the type style, and you can move, reflect, shear, rotate or scale any part or all of the graph.

Creating a graph and importing data

1 Choose New from the File menu.

2 Choose Preferences from the Edit menu. Click Inches for ruler units, and then click OK.

3 Choose Toolbox Options from the View menu and Reset Toolbox from the submenu.

4 Select the Grouped-column-graph tool, and click an inch down from the top-left edge of the screen.

5 Type **4** for Width, type **3** for Height, and click OK.

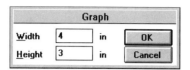

6 From the Graph Data dialog box, choose Import from the File menu.

7 Click the file *8790PDAT.AI*, and click Open.

8 Click OK.

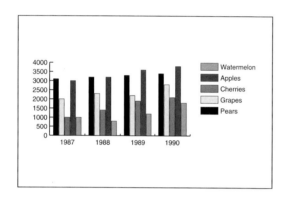

9 Choose Graph Style from the Graph menu, or press Control-Alternate-Shift-S for the Graph Style command.

10 Click Drop Shadow to turn it off.

Editing axis values

1 In the Axis options, click Left, next to Style.

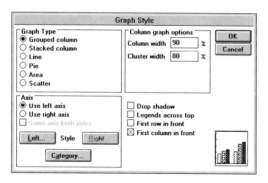

The Graph Axis Style dialog box appears.

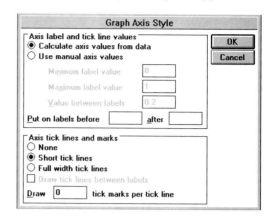

2 Click Use Manual Axis Values. This option lets you enter values for the axis rather than use those that the program generates.

3 Type **5000** for Maximum Label Value.

4 Type **1000** for Value Between Labels.

5 Type **$** for Put On Labels Before.

6 Type **M** for Put On Labels After.

7 Click Full Width Tick Lines under Axis Tick Lines and Marks.

8 Click OK; then click OK again.

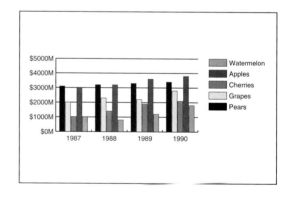

Painting tick lines

1 Choose the Direct-up-selection tool, and click away from the graph to deselect it.

2 Double-click the topmost tick line, the line across the top of the graph.

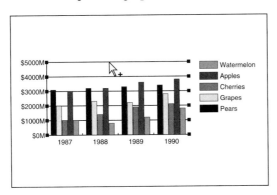

3 Choose Paint Style from the Paint menu.

4 Choose None under Fill.

5 Choose Process Color under Stroke, and type **100** for Cyan.

6 Click Options in the Paint Style dialog box under Dash pattern to change Solid to Dash.

7 Type **5** in the first field, press the Tab key, and type **5** in the second field. Click OK.

8 Click away from the artwork to deselect everything.

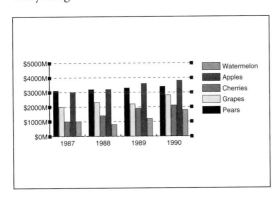

9 Choose Preview Illustration from the View menu.

10 Choose Artwork Only from the View menu.

Changing the font for all of the type

1 Choose Select All from the Edit menu, or press Control-A for the Select All command.

2 Choose Font from the Type menu, and choose GillSans from the Font submenu.

3 Choose Deselect All from the Edit menu.

4 Choose Preview Illustration from the View menu, or press Control-Y for the Preview Illustration command.

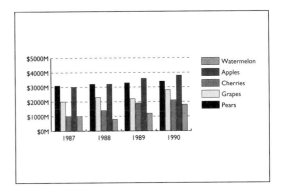

5 Choose Artwork Only from the View menu or press Control-W for the Artwork Only command.

6 Choose Save As from the File menu.

7 Type **8790PROG.AI.**

8 Click OK.

9 Choose Print from the File menu.

10 Choose Close from the File menu.

USING A GRAPH DESIGN TO CUSTOMIZE A GRAPH

You can create custom markers or columns to represent data in a graph. Using a graph design is different from painting a column with a pattern. Graph designs are scaled so that the entire design fits within the column. Once the design is used in the graph, the design can be selected and modified.

Creating a graph and importing data

1 Choose New from the File menu, and click None.

2 Select the Grouped-column-graph tool, and click near the top-left corner of the page.

3 Type **7.5** for Width, type **5.5** for Height, and click OK.

4 From the Graph Data dialog box, choose Import from the File menu.

5 Click the file *87PRODAT.AI*, and click Open.

6 Click OK.

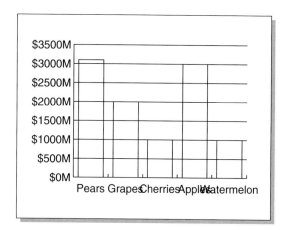

Fitting a graph on the page

1 Choose Fit Artwork in Window from the View menu.

2 Select the Page tool.

3 Position the pointer near the bottom-left corner of the graph; then hold down the mouse button and drag the page boundary until the graph is centered on the page.

Editing text in a graph

1 Select the Zoom-in tool, and click once to zoom in.

2 Choose the Direct-up-selection tool, and click away from the graph to deselect it.

3 Double-click the baseline of the legend name *Watermelon* to select all the legend names.

4 Choose Type Style from the Type menu, type **18** for Size, and click Apply.

5 Double-click the baseline of the legend name *0*.

6 Type **30** for Size, and click OK.

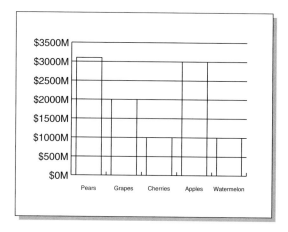

7 Choose Save As from the File menu, or press Control-S for the Save command.

8 Type **87PROGRA.AI**, and click OK.

CREATING A GRAPH DESIGN

You can create custom graph designs from any artwork. The process is similar to creating a pattern in that you first create a bounding rectangle in back of the artwork. Then you define the object as a graph design.

Creating fruit-shape graph designs

1 Choose Open from the File menu, click the file *GCLIPART.AI*, and click Open.

2 Select the Rectangle tool, and click in an empty part of the window.

3 Type **.82** for Width, type **.94** for Height, and click OK.

4 Choose Paint Style from the Paint menu.

5 Choose None under Fill, None under Stroke, and click OK.

6 Choose the Selection tool.

7 Drag the rectangle over the Pear, holding down the Alternate key to make a copy of the rectangle.

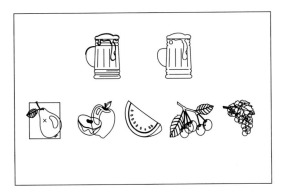

8 Choose Send to Back from the Edit menu.

9 Drag a selection marquee around the rectangle and the pear.

10 Choose Define Graph Design from the Graph menu, or press Control-Alternate-Shift-G for the Define Graph Design command.

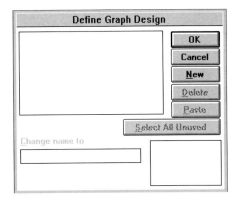

11 Click New, type **Pear**, and click OK.

12 Repeat steps 6–11 to define each of the fruits as a graph design. Remember to copy the bounding rectangle and send it to the back before you define the design. Name the patterns *Apple, Watermelon, Cherries,* and *Grapes,* respectively.

Using the watermelon graph design

1 Choose *87PROGRA.AI* from the Window menu.

2 Choose the Direct-selection tool, and click away from the graph to deselect it.

3 Click the edge of the column above the word *Watermelon.*

4 Choose Use Column Design from the Graph menu, and click Repeating under Column Design Type.

5 Click Watermelon under Column Design Name.

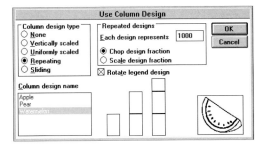

6 Type **1000** for Each Design Represents.

7 Click Chop Design Fraction.

8 Click OK.

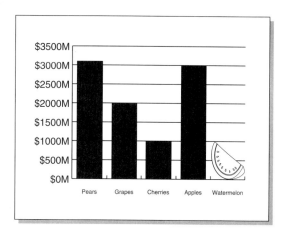

9 Click away from the graph to deselect it.

Using the other fruit graph designs

1 Using the Direct-selection tool, click the edge of the column above Apples.

2 Choose Use Column Design from the Graph menu, and click Repeating under Column Design Type.

3 Click Apples under Column Design Name.

4 Type **1000** for Each Design Represents.

5 Click Chop Design Fraction.

6 Click OK.

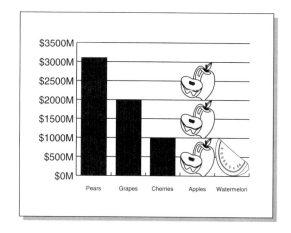

7 Repeat steps 1–6 to fill each column with the appropriate design. Press Control-Alternate-Shift-C to access the Use Column Design dialog.

8 Choose Preview Illustration from the View menu.

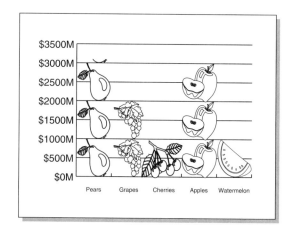

9 Choose Artwork Only from the View menu.

10 Choose Save from the File menu.

11 Choose Print from the File menu.

12 Choose Close from the File menu. (Do not close the *GCLIPART.AI* file.)

CREATING OTHER COLUMN DESIGN TYPES

The program provides several options for displaying column designs. In the sections below, you will experiment with some of those options.

Creating and defining a column design

1 Choose Open from the File menu, and double-click the file named *90RBSALG.AI*.

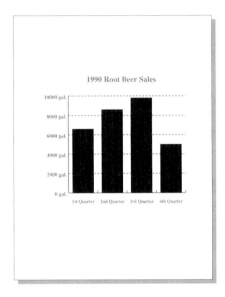

2 Choose *GCLIPART.AI* from the Window menu.

3 Select the Rectangle tool, and click in the window.

4 Type **.94** for Width, type **1.19** for Height, and click OK.

5 Choose the Selection tool, and drag the rectangle over the left root beer mug.

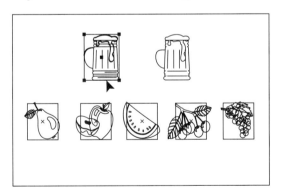

6 Choose Paint Style from the Paint menu.

7 Choose None for Fill, choose None for Stroke, and click OK.

8 Choose Send To Back from the Edit menu, or press Control-Shift-B for the Send To Back command.

9 Using the Selection tool, drag a selection marquee around the root beer mug and the rectangle.

10 Choose Group from the Arrange menu.

11 Choose Define Graph Design from the Graph menu, or Press Control-Alternate-Shift-G for the Define Graph Design command.

12 Click New, type **Root Beer Mug**, and click OK.

Using a vertically scaled design

1 Choose *90RBSALG.AI* from the Window menu. (Make sure that the graph is selected.)

2 Choose Use Column Design from the Graph menu, or press Control-Alternate-Shift-C for the Use Column Design command.

3 Click Vertically Scaled under Column Design Type, click Root Beer Mug under Column Design Name, and click OK.

4 Select the Zoom-out tool, and click once in the center of the graph.

5 Choose Preview Illustration from the View menu.

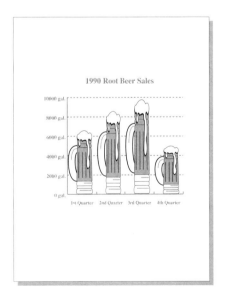

6 Choose Artwork Only from the View menu.

Using a uniformly scaled design

1 Choose Use Column Design from the Graph menu.

2 Click Uniformly Scaled under Column Design Type, click Root Beer Mug under Column Design Name, and click OK.

3 Choose Preview Illustration from the View menu.

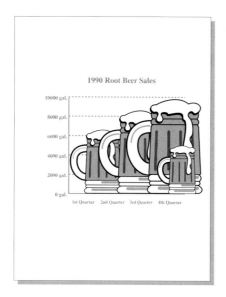

4 Choose Artwork Only from the View menu.

Using a repeating design

1 Choose Use Column Design from the Graph menu.

2 Click Repeating under Column Design Type, and click Root Beer Mug under Column Design Name.

3 Type **2000** for Each Design Represents under Repeated Designs.

4 Click Chop Design Fraction, and click OK.

5 Choose Preview Illustration from the View menu.

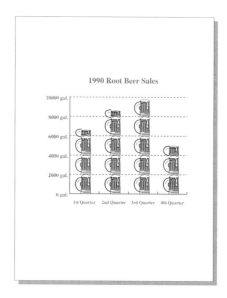

6 Choose Artwork Only from the View menu.

Creating a custom graph with values

1 Choose *GCLIPART.AI* from the Window menu.

2 Choose the Selection tool.

3 Click the leftmost root beer mug to select it.

4 Choose Ungroup from the Arrange menu, or press Control-U for the Ungroup command.

5 Click away from the graphic to deselect it.

6 Select the Type tool, click above the root beer mug, and type **%60**.

7 Double-click the type to select it.

8 Choose Type Style from the Type menu. Type **36** for Size, and click on Centered for alignment. Click OK.

9 Choose Paint Style from the Paint menu.

10 Choose Black for Fill, choose None for Stroke, and click OK.

11 Choose the Selection tool, and drag the *%60* over the bottom of the root beer mug inside the rectangle.

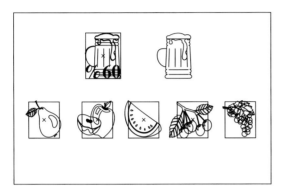

12 Using the Selection tool, drag a selection marquee around the root beer mug and the rectangle.

13 Choose Group from the Arrange menu.

14 Choose Define Graph Design from the Graph menu.

15 Click New, type **Root Beer Mug w/Value**, and click OK.

Displaying graph values

1 Choose *90RBSALG.AI* from the Window menu.

2 Choose Use Column Design from the Graph menu, or press Control-Alternate-Shift-C for the Use Column Design command.

3 Click Vertically Scaled under Column Design Type, click Root Beer Mug w/Value under Column Design Name, and click OK.

4 Choose Deselect All from the Edit menu.

5 Choose Preview Illustration from the View menu.

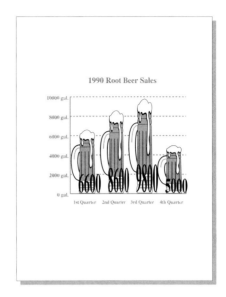

6 Choose Artwork Only from the View menu or press Control-Shift-W for the Artwork Only command.

Creating a sliding graph design

To create a sliding design, you must first define the sliding design boundary, the point from which the design will slide.

1 Choose *GCLIPART.AI* from the Window menu.

2 Select the Rectangle tool, and click in the window.

The values in the Rectangle dialog box should be those of the last rectangle you created: .94 for Width and 1.19 for Height.

3 Click OK.

4 Choose the Selection tool, and drag the rectangle on top of the rightmost root beer mug.

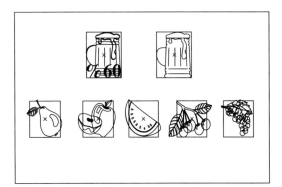

5 Choose Send To Back from the Edit menu, or press Control-Shift-B for the Send To Back command.

6 Select the Zoom-in tool, and click twice on the rightmost root beer mug.

7 Select the Pen tool, position the pointer (an *x*) to the left and just below the handle on the root beer mug, outside the rectangle, and click the mouse button.

8 Position the pointer (a +) outside the right side of the rectangle; then hold down the Shift key and click the mouse button.

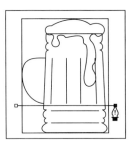

9 Choose the Selection tool, and drag a selection marquee around the root beer mug, the rectangle, and the line running through the rectangle.

10 Choose Group from the Arrange menu, or press Control-G for the Group command.

11 Choose the Direct-up-selection tool, and click away from the artwork to deselect it.

12 Click the line running through the rectangle.

13 Choose Make Guide from the Arrange menu.

14 Choose the Selection tool, and click the root beer mug to select it.

15 Choose Define Graph Design from the Graph menu.

16 Click New, type **Root Beer Mug w/Line**, and click OK.

Using a sliding design

1 Choose *90RBSALG.AI* from the Window menu.

2 Choose Use Column Design from the Graph menu.

3 Click Sliding under Column Design Type, click Root Beer Mug w/Line under Column Design Name, and click OK.

4 Choose Preview Illustration from the View menu.

5 Choose Artwork Only from the View menu.

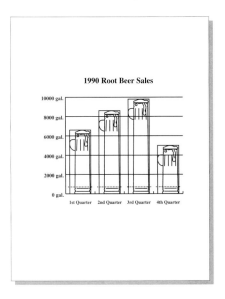

6 Choose Print from the File menu.

7 Close all open files, and do not save changes.

Creating a line graph

1 Choose New from the File menu.

2 Select the Line-graph tool.

3 Click in the upper-left corner of the window.

4 Type **6.5** for Width and **3** for Height, and click OK.

5 Choose Import from the File menu.

6 Click *8890RBDA.AI*, and click Open.

7 Click OK.

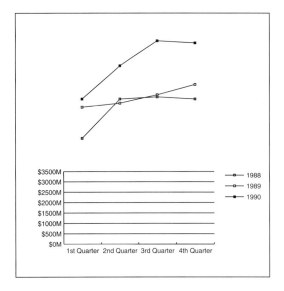

8 Choose Graph Style from the Graph menu.

9 In the Axis options, click Left, next to Style.

10 Click Calculate Axis Values from Data.

11 Delete any existing values from the Put On Labels Before option.

12 Delete any existing values from the Put On Labels After option.

13 Click OK; then click OK again.

14 Choose Preview Illustration from the View menu.

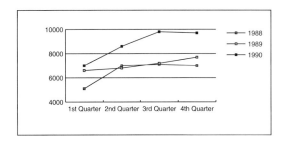

15 Choose Artwork Only from the View menu.

16 Choose Print from the File menu.

17 Choose Close from the File menu. Do not save changes.

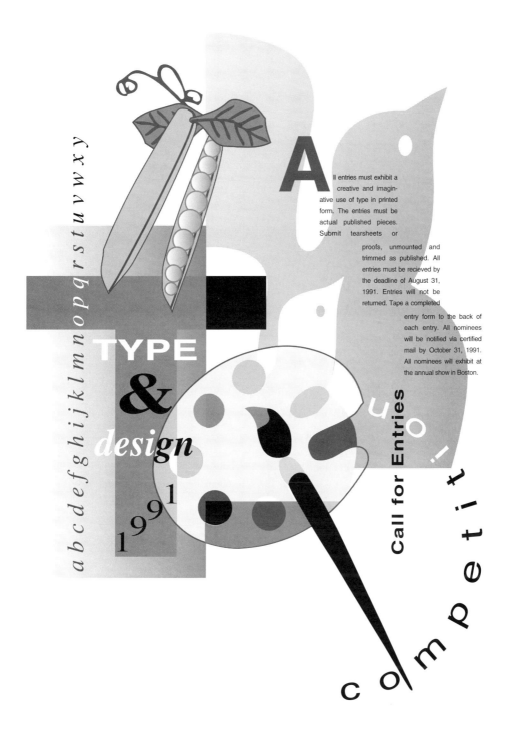

abcdefghijklmnopqrstuvwxy

TYPE
&
design
1991

A
ll entries must exhibit a creative and imaginative use of type in printed form. The entries must be actual published pieces. Submit tearsheets or proofs, unmounted and trimmed as published. All entries must be recieved by the deadline of August 31, 1991. Entries will not be returned. Tape a completed entry form to the back of each entry. All nominees will be notified via certified mail by October 31, 1991. All nominees will exhibit at the annual show in Boston.

Call for Entries

competition!

Lesson

10

LESSON 10: USING OTHER TOOLS AND COMMANDS

In lesson 10, you will have the opportunity to explore some of the other important tools and commands available in the Adobe Illustrator program. The following are some of the included topics:

- Measure tool
- Move command
- Average/Join command
- Hide command
- Creating compound paths
- Creating masks
- Save options

THE MEASURE TOOL

The Measure tool indicates the distance and angle between two points. Such a measurement might be useful before you create, move, or constrain an object. You can measure the distance between endpoints or anchor points on the same path or on different paths, or between any two locations in a blank area of you're artwork.

Using the Measure tool

1 Choose New from the File menu, or press Control-N to open a new file.

2 Select the Pen tool.

3 Click the mouse button in the window. Move the pointer down and right, and click again to draw a diagonal line about 4 inches long.

4 Click the Measure tool.

5 Position the pointer on the top end of the line you just drew, and click the mouse button.

6 Move the pointer to the other end of the line, and click the mouse button again. The Measure dialog box will appear.

Measure		
Distance	4.0235 in	OK
Angle	-44.58 °	
Horizontal	2.8657 in	
Vertical	-2.8242 in	

The distance between the two points appears after Distance. The angle of the line between the two points appears after Angle. The distances between the two points horizontally (along the *x*-axis) and vertically (along the *y*-axis) are also provided.

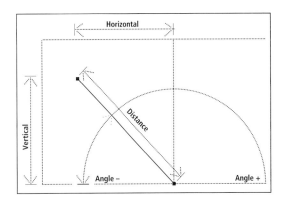

7 Click OK.

MOVING SELECTIONS

You have already moved selected objects visually by dragging them with one of the selection tools. You can also move a selected object a specified distance with the Move command or the arrow keys.

Using the Move command

1 Choose the Object-selection tool, and click the line you just drew to select it.

2 Choose Move from the Edit menu, or press the Alternate key and click the current selection tool to access the Move dialog box. The Move dialog box will appear.

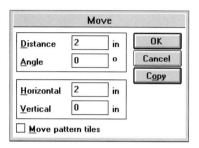

3 Type **2** for Horizontal. Entering a positive number moves the selection up vertically or right horizontally. Entering a negative value moves it down vertically or left horizontally.

4 Click Copy to move a copy of the selected object 2 inches to the right. (If you click OK, you will move the selected object instead of creating a moved copy.)

Moving with the arrow keys

1 Press the Left, Right, Up, and Down Arrow keys on the keyboard to move the line in small increments. The distance that the arrow keys move an object can be set to any amount, but the default is 1 point.

AVERAGING AND JOINING ANCHOR POINTS

You can use the Average and Join commands to reposition and connect anchor points.

Averaging points

The Average command in the Arrange menu brings multiple selected points together at one location that is the average position of all the points selected. You can use the Average command to line up the selected points at their average vertical position, horizontal position, or both.

1 Choose Select All from the Edit menu or press Control-A for the Select All command, and press the Backspace or Delete key to clear the screen.

2 Select the Pen tool, and click to draw two parallel lines of about equal length. (Remember to click the Pen tool in the toolbox to end the first path and begin the second one.)

3 Choose the Selection tool, and drag a selection marquee around one end of each parallel line to select one endpoint of each line.

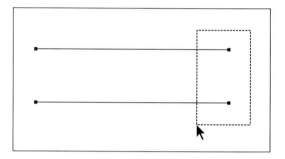

4 Choose Average from the Arrange menu, or press Control-L for the Average command. The Average dialog box will appear.

5 Click OK to average the points along both axes. The two points are moved to their average position.

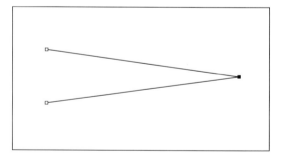

Note: The Average command does not combine the two points; it simply moves them so that one is on top of the other.

Joining points

There are two ways to use the Join command. You can join two points that are on top of each other, or you can join two points by creating a path between them.

1 Choose Join from the Arrange menu, or press Control-J for the Join command. (The two points you averaged in the last step should still be selected.) The Join dialog box appears.

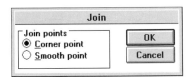

2 Click OK to accept the defaults. The two selected points are now a single point.

3 Use the Pen tool to draw two more parallel lines. (Remember to click the Pen tool in the toolbox after you draw the first path.)

4 Choose the Selection tool, and drag a selection marquee around one end of each parallel line.

5 Choose Join from the Arrange menu. The endpoints will be connected with a straight line.

EXAMINING THE LOCK COMMAND

The Lock command in the Arrange menu causes any selected paths to be temporarily unselectable. This greatly reduces your chance of accidentally editing a finished portion of your illustration while you are working on an unfinished area. All the locked paths can be made selectable and editable once again with the Unlock All command.

Note that you cannot lock a portion of a path or a part of a group, you must lock the entire path or group.

EXAMINING THE HIDE COMMAND

The Hide command in the Arrange menu causes any selected paths to be temporarily invisible. This greatly reduces the amount of time it takes the program to redraw, preview, or print the illustration. The hidden paths can be made visible again with the Show All command. Hiding objects is temporary and is not saved with the illustration. When you reopen a file containing objects you have previously hidden, you will see all the objects.

EXAMINING THE HIDE UNPAINTED OBJECTS COMMAND

The Hide Unpainted Objects command in the View menu causes all unfilled, unstroked paths to be hidden. You can show them again by choosing Show Unpainted Objects from the View menu.

When you draw a text rectangle with the Type tool, the path is unfilled and unstroked. You can use the Hide Unpainted Objects command to hide the paths in Artwork mode.

SETTING CROP MARKS

The Adobe Illustrator program lets you set the position of crop marks on a page. Crop marks will print from the Adobe Illustrator program, or from the Adobe Separator program if you plan to separate your color Adobe Illustrator documents. Setting crop marks in the Adobe Illustrator program actually defines the bounding box that the Adobe Separator program uses to print.

Note: If you plan to separate your color Adobe Illustrator documents using the Adobe Separator program, you should first set crop marks using the Adobe Illustrator program; if you want to reposition the crop marks, you can do this using the Adobe Separator program. You cannot create more than one set of crop marks in a file.

To set crop marks:

1 Select the Rectangle tool.

2 Click and release the mouse button. Type **3** for width and **5** for height. Click OK.

3 Choose Set Crop marks from the Arrange menu.

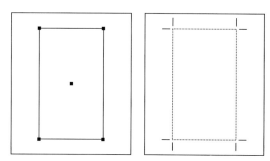

4 Choose Release Crop marks from the Arrange menu.

USING THE PAGE LAYOUT COMMAND

The Print Setup dialog box under the File menu allows you to select the paper size and the orientation, either tall (portrait) or wide (landscape), and it offers several other options.

Use the Paper Size pop-up list to choose a paper size.

THE PAGE TOOL

The Page tool allows you to reposition the page boundaries relative to the artwork (instead of moving all the selected paths around on the page).

Using the Page tool

1 Choose Fit Artwork In Window from the View menu.

2 Select the Page tool.

3 Position the pointer on the bottom-left corner of the page grid; then hold down the mouse button and drag the page boundary to reposition it relative to the artwork.

4 When the page is repositioned, release the mouse button.

5 Choose Close from the File menu. Do not save changes.

USING THE PLACE COMMAND

The Place command allows you to include any PostScript language file in your illustration, including scanned artwork saved in Encapsulated PostScript (EPS) format, other Adobe Illustrator files, and EPS output from other applications that can save in this format.

Using the Place command

1 Choose New fro m the File menu, or press Control-N to open a new file.

2 Choose Place Art from the File menu, and double-click the file named *PHOTO.EPS*.

3 Choose Preview Illustration from the View menu, or press Control-Y for the Preview Illustration command, to see the image in bitmapped form. It will look like the one shown below, except that it will be in color on a color monitor or on a color printer equipped with a PostScript interpreter.

You can edit placed files only by moving, copying, scaling, rotating, reflecting, and shearing.

4 Choose Close from the File menu, or press Control-W for the Artwork Only command. Do not save changes.

USING COMPOUND PATHS

You can use compound paths to create a window effect in layers of artwork. When you create a compound path, you can "see through" one layer to another. The effect is similar to that of cutting a hole in a paint layer so you can see what is behind it.

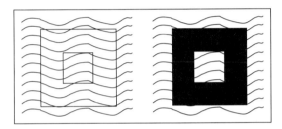

If parts of a compound path do not overlap, you see a reverse or knockout effect, as shown.

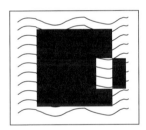

Type outlines are created by the program as compound paths. This allows you to see through the counters in the letters.

For example, you see through the middle of the D.

If you select a compound path and choose Release Compound from the Paint menu, the see-through effect is removed, and both paths are filled.

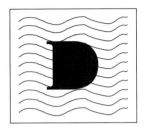

As you have seen, the Adobe Illustrator program paints your artwork by applying successive layers of opaque paint to the objects. Each layer obscures the layer behind it. Compound paths, in effect, let you create holes in the layers of paint so that you can see through one layer to a background layer. In most cases, when compound paths overlap, a hole appears.

Creating a filled rectangle layer

In this part of the lesson, you will edit while viewing your work in preview mode.

1 Choose New from the File menu.

2 Choose Toolbox Options from the View menu and Reset Toolbox from the submenu.

3 Select the Rectangle tool, and draw a rectangle about 3 inches by 2 inches in the middle of your screen.

4 Choose Paint Style from the Paint menu, or press Control-I for the Paint Style command.

5 Choose Black under Fill, and type **50**.

6 Choose Black under Stroke, and type **2** for Weight.

7 Choose Preview Illustration from the View menu.

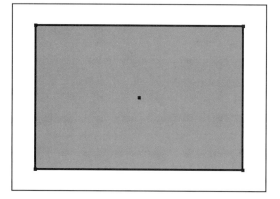

Creating a second rectangle layer

1 Select the Scale-dialog tool, and click the center of the rectangle.

2 Type **50** for Uniform Scale, and click Copy.

Creating a third layer

1 Select the Oval tool; then hold down the Shift key and draw a small circle that overlaps the bottom left corner of the inner rectangle.

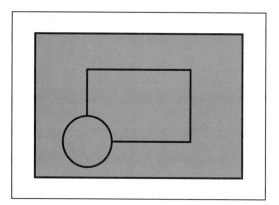

2 Choose Paint Style from the Paint menu or press Control-I for the Paint Style command.

3 Choose Process Color under Fill. Type **100** for Cyan, **100** for Yellow, and **None** for Stroke, and click OK.

4 Choose Send to Back from the Edit menu or press Control-Shift-B for the Send to Back command.

Notice that you do not see all of the circle.

Creating a compound path

1 Choose the Selection tool, and click away from the artwork to deselect everything.

2 Click the edge of one of the rectangles to select it.

3 Hold down the Shift key and click the edge of the other rectangle to add it to the selection.

4 Choose Make Compound from the Paint menu, or press Control-Alternate-G for the Make Compound command.

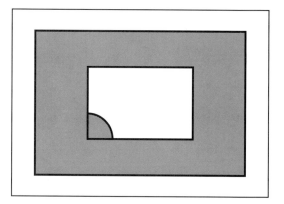

Because the rectangles are a compound path, you see the circle on the bottom layer through the inner rectangle.

5 Use the Selection tool to drag the rectangles around the window.

Notice that the rectangles are grouped and that you can see the circle through any position inside the inner rectangle.

USING MASKS

Using a masking path is another way to create special layering effects.

1 Choose Select All from the Edit menu, or press Control-A for the Select All command.

2 Press the Backspace or Delete key to delete all the artwork.

Creating and painting an oval

First you will create an oval as a regular path.

1 Select the Oval tool, and click in the center of the window. The Oval dialog box will appear.

2 Type **3** for Width and **2** for Height, and click OK.

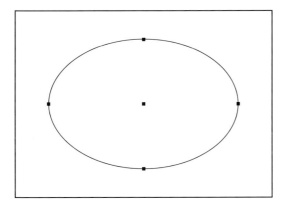

3 Choose Ungroup from the Arrange menu, or press Control-U for the Ungroup command.

4 Choose Artwork Only from the View Menu.

5 Choose the Selection tool.

6 Click away from the artwork to deselect everything.

7 Click to select the center point.

8 Press the Backspace or Delete key to erase the center point.

9 Click the edge of the oval to select it.

10 Choose Paint Style from the Paint menu or press Control-I for the Paint Style command. Choose None under Fill. Choose None under Stroke, and click OK.

11 Choose Preview Illustration from the View menu.

Creating and painting several rectangles

Next you will create several rectangles that will become the masked objects.

1 Select the Centered-rectangle tool.

2 Click the leftmost anchor point of the oval. The Rectangle dialog box will appear.

3 Type **.5** for Width and **2.5** for Height, and click OK.

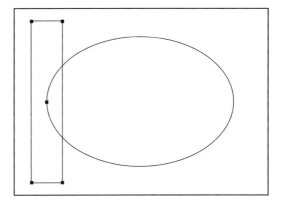

4 Choose Paint Style from the Paint menu. Choose Black under Fill and None under Stroke, and click OK.

5 Choose Move from the Edit menu.

6 Type **.8** for Horizontal, and click Copy.

7 Choose Transform Again from the Arrange menu, or press Control-D three times for the Transform Again command to make more copies of the rectangle.

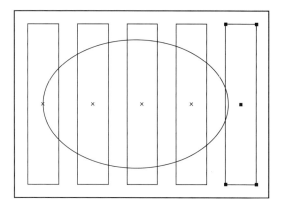

The oval is hidden and has no effect on the rectangle.

Making the oval a masking path

Finally you make the oval a masking path. Note that a masking path applies only to objects that are within its boundaries and in front of the masking path in the painting order.

1 Choose the Object-selection tool.

2 Drag a small selection marquee in the area between two black rectangles to select the oval. Make sure that you have not selected any of the rectangles.

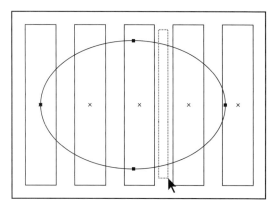

3 Choose Paint Style from the Paint menu, or press Control-I for the Paint Style command.

4 Click the Mask checkbox and move it to the edge of your screen. Click Apply, then OK.

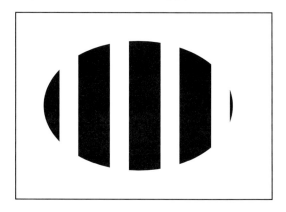

You now see that the oval is a masking path that masks or hides everything that is outside of it and in front of it.

5 Drag a selection marquee around all of the rectangles and the oval to select them.

6 Choose Group from the Arrange menu.

Note: *Always group the masking path with the masked objects.*

When you group a masking path (the oval) with the objects in front of it, the mask applies only to those objects. Everything else in the artwork is unaffected by the mask.

Rules for masking

• The masking path itself must be ungrouped. If it is a rectangle or an oval, it must be ungrouped, and the center point must be removed.

• The masking path must be behind the objects it will mask.

• The masking path should be grouped with the objects to be masked. In this lesson, you grouped the oval with the rectangles. If you do not group the masking path with objects to be masked, other objects in the illustration that are outside the masking path and behind the masking path may not preview or print.

• Only one path or shape can be a masking path for a particular group of objects (one oval for the rectangles).

EXAMINING CAPS AND JOINS

This section reviews some of the other options in the Paint Style dialog box.

1 Choose Paint Style from the Paint menu, or press Control-I for the Paint Style command, so you can see the Paint Style dialog box.

2 Click Options.

Line caps

The Caps option determines the appearance of the endpoints of open paths and the ends of dash segments in dashed lines. Such endpoints can be treated in any one of the three ways shown.

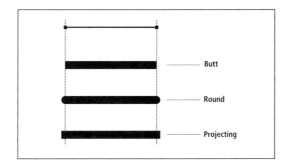

Line joins

The Joins option determines the appearance of the corners of stroked paths. You can use any of the three types of line joins shown. Joins do not affect endpoints; they affect only anchor points that occur within a path between endpoints. The Joins option has no effect where stroked paths intersect.

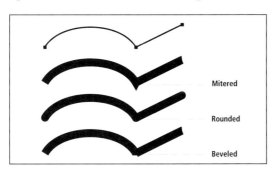

Line pattern

This feature allows you to create dashed or dotted lines by specifying a pattern of dashes and gaps in a stroke.

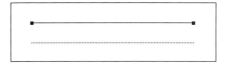

EXAMINING THE FLATNESS OPTION

Flatness affects the quality of previewed and printed images. Under normal circumstances, flatness is set to 0 pixels, and you need not change it. However, if you need to speed up preview or printing at the cost of line resolution and accuracy, set the flatness to 1 or greater. If you have limited memory in your computer, and your illustration is complex, the program may inform you that you need to set the flatness to greater than 1 when previewing long paths.

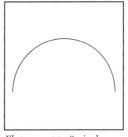 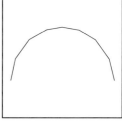

Flatness set to 0 pixels   *Flatness set to 20 pixels*

EXAMINING THE NOTE OPTION

The Note option lets you enter an annotation for artwork objects. Annotated objects are useful for PostScript language programmers who will be using a text editor to modify the code produced by the Adobe Illustrator program. With annotation, particular objects in an illustration can be quickly located within the code.

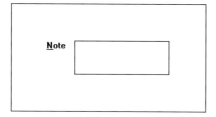

EXAMINING THE SAVE OPTIONS

1 Click Cancel to close the Paint Style dialog box.

2 Choose Save As from the File menu to see the Save As dialog box.

Saving documents

Save your document frequently as you work. Do not wait until your artwork is complete, or you may have to redo your work if you experience a system error or a power failure. To save your document, use the Save command under the File menu.

When the program saves a document, with a template, the program also saves a path name to the template. The program does not save the template itself, because it is stored as a separate document. If you move the artwork document and template to a new directory or disk, you must place the template again and save it with the document to update the path name. If you do not update the path name, the artwork document may not be able to locate the template. To save a document as a template, save it as a TIFF (*.TIFF*), PCX (*.PCX*), or BMP (*.BMP*) file.

Compatibility with Adobe Illustrator 3.0, 88, and 1.1 program versions

You may want to save an Adobe Illustrator document for use on a Macintosh or a NeXT computer or some other platform on which the Adobe Illustrator program is available—or with another application that reads the Adobe Illustrator format. To save a document as an Adobe Illustrator 3.0, Adobe Illustrator 88, or Adobe Illustrator 1.1 document, select the appropriate option in the Compatibility list box in the Save As dialog box.

Keep in mind that if you save a document in one of these formats, some features will not be available. For example, in Adobe Illustrator 1.1 format, custom colors are converted to process colors, masking is not in effect (although all objects involved in the mask are present), and patterns and all placed images are removed. In Adobe Illustrator 88 format, compound paths, guide objects, grids, and most text features are saved in a modified form.

Saving documents with an EPSF header

You can specify three different file formats when saving a document; to do so, you use the Preview field in the Save As dialog box. All of the formats automatically save the document as an Encapsulated PostScript (*.EPS*) file with a Tag Image File Format (TIFF) preview and with an EPSF header. By default, the program appends the *.AI* extension to a document name.

The EPSF header enables you to open the document in the Adobe Separator program, if you plan to separate your color document using this application, or to export your document to another application. If you want to use your document as a PostScript file in other applications, use the *.EPS* extension when saving a document.

Standard (No Preview) is the default Save format. Saving your document in this format lets you use the document on the Macintosh computer, NeXT Computer, or DEC Workstation, or on other platforms on which the Adobe Illustrator program runs; however, you cannot preview your document.

The Color and Black & White formats save the document for use on the PC only, and they allow you to preview the document as a TIFF (.*TIFF*) file. The Color format saves the document as 256 colors; the Black & White format saves the document in black and white.

If you know how to program in the PostScript language, you can also open documents saved in the Include EPSF Header format with any word processor and make changes to them; however, you should take certain precautions before editing Adobe Illustrator program documents. Some modifications of the PostScript language document will cause the document to be unopenable, although you will still be able to place it or print it. When you are not sure about the effects of a change you want to make, check with the following Adobe Systems documentation, published by Addison-Wesley: *PostScript Language Program Design, PostScript Language Tutorial and Cookbook,* and *PostScript Language Reference Manual.*

Saving documents with placed or pasted images

If you have placed Encapsulated PostScript (EPS) images in the document you are saving, and you will be using the document with page layout applications, click the Include Placed Images options in the Save As dialog box. This option is available only when you have placed EPS images in your document. This saves a copy of the placed images with your Adobe Illustrator file.

Using the Adobe Illustrator EPSF Rider files

The *RIDERS.AI* file is included with your application on the Tutorial and Gallery disk. This file is intended only for users who are fluent in the Adobe PostScript language. If you are not an experienced PostScript language user, you should not use this file. If you use this file, place it into the directory with the Adobe Illustrator application. If you are not using the file, do not place it into the directory with the Adobe Illustrator application, because the *RIDERS.AI* file can slow down the program's performance.

If you are an experienced PostScript user, you can add PostScript fragments to the *RIDERS.AI* file. This file allows you to customize your Adobe Illustrator files. For example, you can insert your company logo so that it appears on all of your documents. You can also use the file to set screen angles and frequencies for your documents.

The PostScript language fragments you enter in the *RIDERS.AI* file are saved with the document when you print it or save it with an EPSF header. The PostScript language fragments you enter in the *RIDERS.AI* file are also inserted when you print a document. If you use the *RIDERS.AI* file to customize your documents and then later open one of your documents using someone else's application, your *RIDERS.AI* file will be overwritten by the other person's rider file.

You can enter PostScript language fragments in each of four sections: comments, prolog, setup, and trailer. For information on using these four sections, refer to *Adobe Illustrator Document Format,* available from Adobe Systems' Developer Support.

Note: Be aware that the PostScript language fragments you enter in the Adobe Illustrator EPSF Riders file can affect printing. If you encounter printing difficulties, check to make sure that you have not made errors entering PostScript code.

EXAMINING THE PREFERENCES DIALOG BOX

1 Click Cancel to close the Save As dialog box.

2 Choose Preferences from the Edit menu.

The Preferences dialog box allows you to set a number of parameters that affect various operations in the Adobe Illustrator program. This feature allows you to configure the program the way that you prefer. Settings remain in effect until you change them.

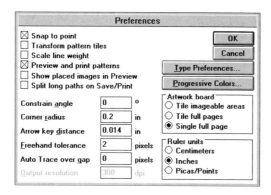

Snap To Point

When this option is on, any selected point that is moved to within two pixels of another point will gravitate to that point.

Transform Pattern Tiles

When this option is on, any patterns used in the illustration will be affected by the transformation operations (rotating, scaling, shearing, and reflecting). When this option is off, objects that are filled with a pattern will be transformed, but the pattern itself will not be transformed.

Scale Line Weight

When this option is on, the Scale Line Weight option of the Scale dialog box is always on as a default.

Preview and Print Patterns

When this option is on, any patterns used in the illustration will be displayed when you preview and print. When this option is off, patterns are ignored, saving time during previewing and printing operations.

Show Placed Images

When this option is on, any placed images in the document will be displayed when you preview. When this option is off, placed images are represented as outlined boxes with diagonal lines.

Split Long Paths On Save/Print

This option causes the program to split any paths that are too large to print at the resolution you specify with the Output Resolution option. Unless you experience problems printing complicated shapes, you should leave this option off.

Constrain Angle

This option sets the angle along which the Shift key's constraining action will occur. Normally the Constrain Angle is set to 0 degrees, which causes the Shift key to constrain operations to multiples of 45 degrees. Shift key constraining affects moving, copying, and transformations, as well as actions of the Rectangle, Oval, Pen, and Type tools.

Corner Radius

This option determines how rounded the corners will be on rectangles drawn with the Rectangle tool. When the value is zero, the corners are squared.

Arrow Key Distance

This option sets the distance that selections will move when the arrow keys on the keyboard are pressed.

Freehand Tolerance

This option determines how sensitive the Freehand tool is to variations in your hand movement. Measured in pixels, the Freehand Tolerance can be set from 1 to 10. The higher the number, the smoother the resulting lines and curves will be.

Autotrace Over Gap

This option sets the number of pixels across which the Auto Trace tool will jump on a template when you are autotracing. The value can be set from 0 to 2 pixels. If a template is rough and has gaps, setting this number at 2 pixels may smooth it out. However, you may lose some fine details at the higher setting.

Output Resolution

This option is available only when you choose Split Long Paths with the Save/Print option. If you use that option, you must enter your printer resolution in the Output Resolution field.

Type Preferences

This dialog box lets you change the units in which type attributes are measured.

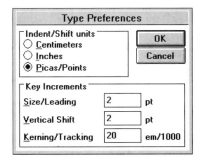

Indent/Shift units can be centimeters, inches, or picas/points.

Key Increments sets the increments used for keyboard shortcuts.

Progressive Colors

This option allows you to adjust the displayed colors on your color monitor (or shades of gray on a monochrome monitor) so that they match the printed colors. Resetting these colors does not affect printed color.

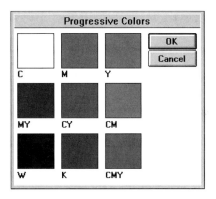

Artwork Board

The Artwork Board options determine how the artwork area is *tiled*, or divided, when printed. Because the artwork board is 18 inches by 18 inches, the area is subdivided into printer-sized pages when printed. Tiling depends on the paper size you select in the Page Layout dialog box.

Tile Imageable Areas divides the artwork board into pages, with gray lines defining the printable surface of each page. The number of pages depends on the paper size you have selected. The most common setting (U.S. letter-sized paper printed at 100 percent) divides the document into nine pages.

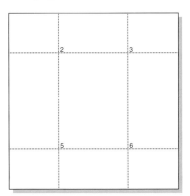

Ruler Units

This option lets you select the units of measurement in the program as centimeters, inches, or picas/points. These are the units you see when you choose the Show Rulers command. Most of the dialog boxes will use these units. Be aware that when this setting is Picas/Points, the dialog boxes use points, and the rulers use picas.

Single Full Page creates one page.

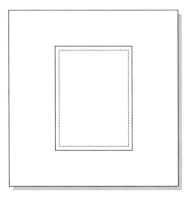

Tile Full Pages lets you use the Page tool to arrange as many full-sized pages on the artwork board as your printer can print.

Click Cancel to close the Preferences dialog box.

Creating two full pages

1 Close any open artwork windows. Do not save changes.

2 Choose New from the File menu.

3 Choose Preferences from the Edit menu.

4 Click Tile Full Pages under Artwork Board, and then click OK.

5 Choose Print Setup from the File menu

6 Click Portrait for Orientation, and click OK.

7 Choose Fit Artwork In Window from the View menu.

8 Select the Page tool.

9 Position the pointer near the bottom-left corner of the rectangles, near the *1*.

10 Hold down the mouse button and drag to the left. When the pointer is near the left edge of the page, release the mouse button. You will see two full pages.

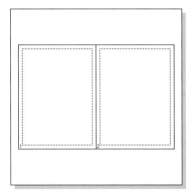

Note that if you are working in landscape mode, you can position two pages one above the other rather than side-by-side.

11 Choose Actual Size from the View menu. Notice the page boundaries on the page.

12 Choose Close from the File menu. Do not save changes.

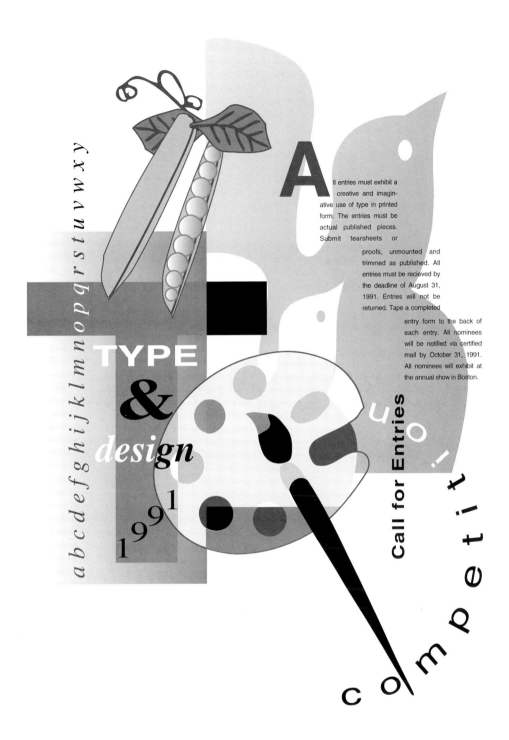

a b c d e f g h i j k l m n o p q r s t u v w x y

TYPE

&

design

1991

A

All entries must exhibit a creative and imaginative use of type in printed form. The entries must be actual published pieces. Submit tearsheets or proofs, unmounted and trimmed as published. All entries must be recieved by the deadline of August 31, 1991. Entries will not be returned. Tape a completed entry form to the back of each entry. All nominees will be notified via certified mail by October 31, 1991. All nominees will exhibit at the annual show in Boston.

Call for Entries

c o m p e t i t i o n

Lesson

11

LESSON 11: MASK BOOK COVER

This lesson is a directed study project designed to give you an opportunity to practice the concepts that were covered in lesson 7–10 and earlier.

In this lesson, you will create this book cover.

You will begin by tracing a template to create the mask artwork. Next you will create the rectangles for the book and use a transformed pattern as a fill. Finally you will add type to complete the book cover.

CREATING THE MASK ARTWORK

You begin by using a template to draw the mask artwork. Then you paint the path and save the file.

Drawing the mask artwork

1 Choose New from the File menu.

2 Choose Preferences from the Edit menu, click Single Full Page, and click OK.

3 Choose Place Template from the File menu. Double-click the file called *MASKTMP.TIF*, and click OK.

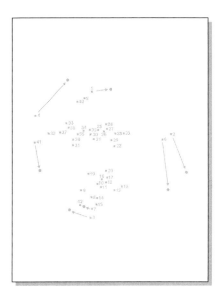

You will use the Pen tool to create a single, continuous path using the template as a guide.

Take a moment to examine the template and notice the numbers. Point 1 is near the top center of the template, point 2 is on the right side of the template, point 3 is near the bottom center, point 4 is near the top left, and point 5 is just below point 1.

You will create both straight lines and curved lines with the Pen tool. Wherever you see an isolated square, you will click the mouse button. Wherever you see an anchor point with an arrow pointing to a circle, you will hold down the mouse button on the square and drag to the circle, thus creating a curved segment. At points 1 through 4, for example, you hold down the mouse button and drag following the arrow.

4 Scroll until you can see point 1 of the template on your screen.

5 Select the Pen tool.

6 Press the Space bar for access to the Hand tool to move through the template, and position the pointer on point 1 of the template.

7 Hold down the mouse button and drag to the circle at the end of the arrow. Then release the mouse button.

8 Move the pointer to point 2; then hold down the mouse button and drag to the circle. Release the mouse button.

9 Continue this process until you get to point 5, where you click instead of drag.

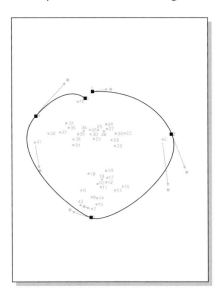

10 Use the Zoom-in tool whenever you want to change the view.

11 Continue drawing lines and curves until you reach the final point (point 42).

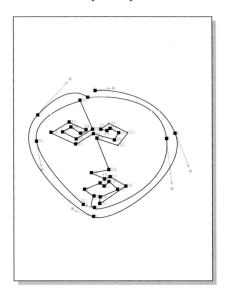

12 Click the Pen tool to end the path.

Remember that if you make a mistake, you can choose Undo from the Edit menu to undo your last action. If you delete a line segment, you must click on the last anchor point with the Pen tool and then continue.

Painting the mask artwork

1 Choose Select All from the Edit menu, or press Control-A for the Select All command.

2 Set the paint attributes as follows:

   Fill: Custom Color, Mask Red
   Stroke: Black
   Weight: 6.5

Click Option, and click Solid under Dash pattern.

3 Choose Preview Illustration from the View menu, or press Control-Y for the Preview Illustration command.

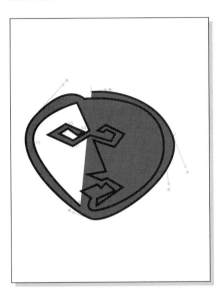

4 Choose Artwork & Template from the View menu.

5 Choose Save As from the File menu.

6 Type **MASKART.AI,** and click OK.

7 Choose Close from the File menu.

CREATING THE BOOK ARTWORK

Next you will draw and paint the rectangles for the book.

Creating and painting the rectangles

1 Choose New from the File menu.

2 Choose Preferences from the Edit menu.

3 Click Inches under Ruler Units, and click OK.

4 Select the Zoom-out tool, and click once in the window.

5 Select the Rectangle tool, and click near the upper-left corner of the window.

6 Type **6** for Width, type **8** for Height, and click OK.

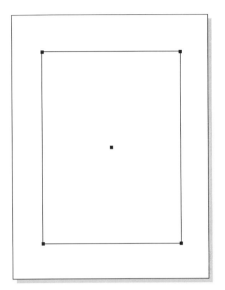

7 Choose Fit Artwork In Window from the View menu, or press Control-M for the Fit In Window command.

8 Choose Move from the Edit menu.

9 Type **-0.07** for Horizontal, type **-0.07** for Vertical, and click Copy.

10 Choose Transform Again from the Arrange menu, or press Control-D three times.

You should now have five rectangles.

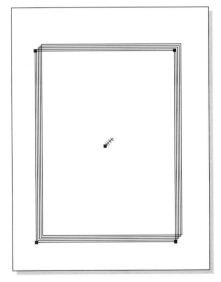

11 Choose Select All from the Edit menu.

12 Set the paint attributes as follows:

  Fill: White
  Stroke: Black
  Weight: 1

Adding a line to the book cover

1 Select the Zoom-in tool.

2 Click three times near the top-left corner of the rectangles to zoom in.

3 Select the Pen tool.

4 Position the pointer on the top-left corner of the leftmost rectangle, and click the mouse button.

5 Move the pointer to the top-left corner of the rightmost rectangle, and click the mouse button.

6 Click the Pen tool to end the path.

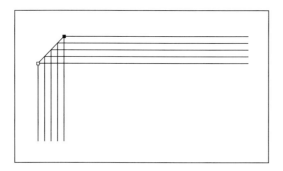

7 Choose Save As from the File menu.

8 Type **BOOKART.AI**, and click OK.

Painting the book cover with a pattern

Next you will transform a pattern and use it to paint a rectangle.

1 Choose the Selection tool.

2 Click the leftmost rectangle to select it.

3 Choose Paint Style from the Paint menu, or press Control-I for the Paint Style command.

4 Choose Pattern under Fill.

5 Choose Mask Pattern in the pattern list.

6 Click Transform.

7 Type **20** for Rotate Angle, and click OK. Then click OK.

Adding the mask artwork to the book cover

1 Choose Open from the File menu, and double-click the file named *MASKART.AI.*

2 Choose Select All from the Edit menu, or press Control-A for the Select All command.

3 Choose Group from the Arrange menu.

4 Choose Copy from the Edit menu.

5 Choose Close from the File menu. Do not save changes.

6 Choose Paste from the Edit menu.

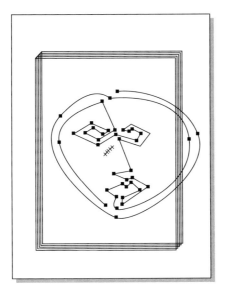

7 Select the Scale-dialog tool.

8 Click the anchor point at the bottom of the mask.

9 Type **60** for Uniform Scale, and click OK.

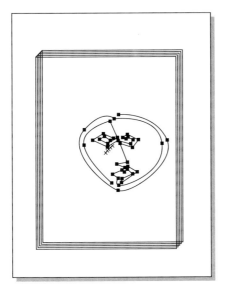

10 Choose Actual Size from the View menu.

11 Choose the Selection tool.

12 Position the mask artwork on the book cover, as shown below.

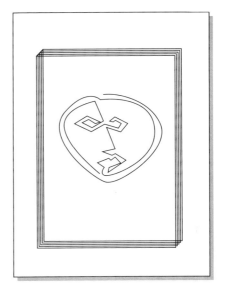

13 Choose the Zoom-out tool, and click once.

14 Choose Preview Illustration from the View menu.

15 Choose Artwork Only from the View menu.

ADDING TYPE TO THE BOOK COVER

Finally you will add type to the book cover. First you will draw a large curved path for the type.

Drawing a path

1 Select the Pen tool.

2 Position the pointer 1 inch outside the left edge of the mask near the eye, and drag upward.

3 Move the pointer to the right edge of the mask at about the same height as the first point, and drag downward.

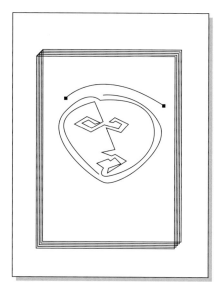

Creating type on a path

1 Select the Type tool.

2 Position the pointer near the beginning of the curve. Watch for the pointer to change to an I-beam with a jagged line.

3 Click the mouse button.

4 Type **Ceremony**.

5 Double-click to select the word *Ceremony.*

6 Set the type attributes as follows:

Font: Times
Size: 95
Leading: 95
Tracking: 100
Horiz. Scale: 60

7 Set the paint attributes as follows:

Fill: Process Color, Y-100
Stroke: None

8 Click the Type tool in the toolbox to end the text block.

9 Choose the Selection tool, and adjust the word *Ceremony* until it appears centered over the mask on the curve.

Creating type at a specified point

1 Select the Type tool, and position the I-beam pointer 1 inch below the center of the mask artwork.

2 Type:

and
Ritual
B. L. PEARSON

Put a carriage return at the end of each line.

3 Click the Selection tool to select the baseline of the text.

4 Choose Alignment from the Type menu and Left from the submenu.

5 With the Type tool, drag to select the word *and*.

6 Choose Type Style from the Type menu, or press Control-T for the Type Style command.

7 Type **48** for Size, and click Apply.

8 Drag to select *B. L. Pearson*.

9 Set the type attributes as follows:

Font: GillSans
Size: 18
Leading: 18.5
Tracking: 90
Horiz. Scale: 100

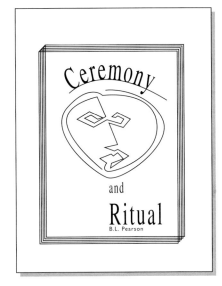

10 With the Type tool, drag to select *Ritual* and *B.L. Pearson*.

11 Type **25** for Vertical Shift, and click OK.

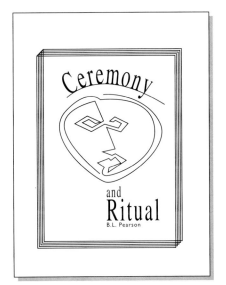

12 Choose the Selection tool to select the baseline of the text.

13 Reposition the type object inside the bottom-right edge of the book.

14 Choose Preview Illustration from the View menu.

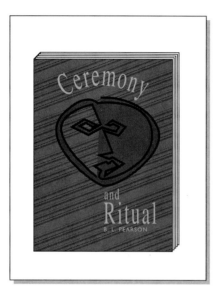

15 Choose Artwork Only from the View menu.

16 Choose Save from the File menu.

17 Choose Print from the File menu.

18 Choose Close from the File menu.

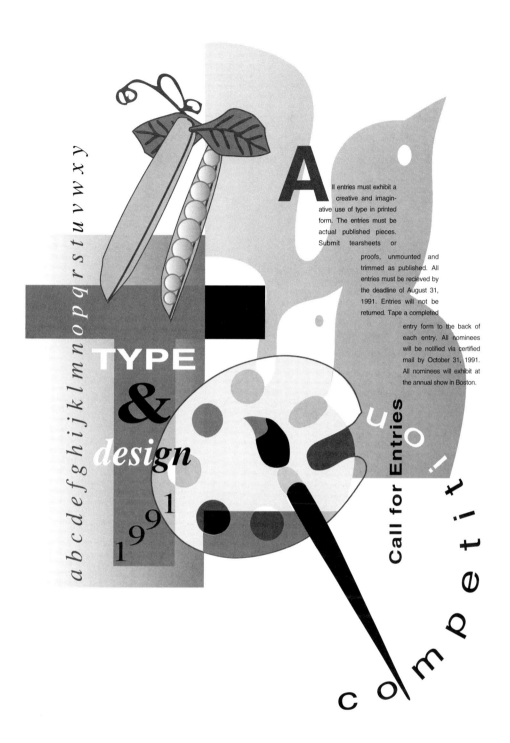

a b c d e f g h i j k l m n o p q r s t u v w x y

TYPE

&

design

1991

A

ll entries must exhibit a creative and imagin-ative use of type in printed form. The entries must be actual published pieces. Submit tearsheets or proofs, unmounted and trimmed as published. All entries must be recieved by the deadline of August 31, 1991. Entries will not be returned. Tape a completed entry form to the back of each entry. All nominees will be notified via certified mail by October 31, 1991. All nominees will exhibit at the annual show in Boston.

Call for **Entries**

competition!

Lesson

12

Lesson 12: Bay Reporter Layout

This lesson is a directed study project designed to give you an opportunity to practice the concepts that were covered in lessons 7–11 and earlier.

In this lesson, you will create this one-page layout for the *Bay Reporter*.

The text and graphics for the project have already been created in separate files. You will import the text and then copy and paste the graphic elements to lay out the newsletter.

Copying and pasting the fish

1 Choose Open from the File menu. Double-click the file named *BRGUIDE.AI* to open the file.

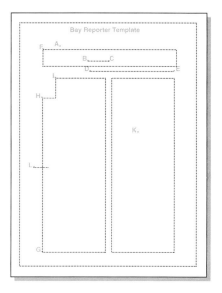

2 Choose Open from the File menu, and double-click the file named *FISHART.AI* to open it.

3 Choose Select All from the Edit menu, or press Control-A for the Select All command.

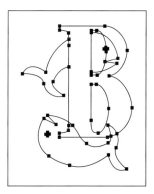

4 Choose Copy from the Edit menu.

5 Choose Close from the File menu to close the Fish Art file.

6 Choose Paste from the Edit menu.

7 Choose the Selection tool.

8 Position the pointer on the leftmost fish fin, and drag up to point A.

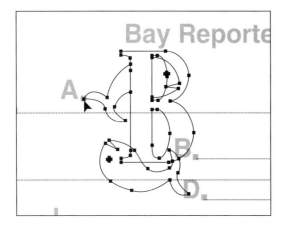

9 Choose Save As from the File menu.

10 Type **BREPART.AI**, and click Save.

Creating the headline

1 Select the Zoom-in tool, and click once near the fish artwork.

2 Select the Type tool, and click point B.

3 Type **ay**.

4 Click the Type tool.

5 Click point C.

6 Type **Reporter**.

7 Click any tool in the toolbox. The text object is selected when you click a tool in the toolbox.

8 Use the Up and Down Arrow keys on the keyboard to line up the baseline of *Reporter* with the baseline of *ay*.

9 Choose the Selection tool.

10 Hold down the Shift key and click *ay* to select both type objects.

11 Set the type attributes as described below. Remember to apply the attributes.

Font: Helvetica-Bold
Size: 42
Tracking: 100
Vertical Shift: 0
Alignment: Left

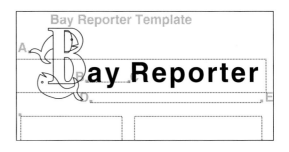

12 Set the paint attributes as described below. Remember to apply the attributes.

Fill: Process Color, C-60, M-20, Y-50, K-0

Creating the subheads

1 Select the Type tool, and click point D. The type you are about to create will be large because it is the same size as the last type created.

2 Type (in all capital letters):

VOLUME TWO, NUMBER ONE

3 Choose Select All from the Edit menu.

4 Set the type attributes as follows:

Font: Helvetica
Size: 10
Tracking: 0

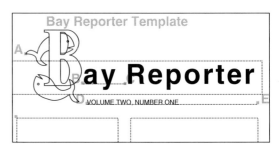

5 Choose Actual Size from the View menu.

6 Click the Type tool in the toolbox.

7 Click point E.

8 Type (in all capital letters):

THREE DOLLARS

9 Choose Select All from the Edit menu.

10 Set the type attributes as follows:

Tracking: 0
Alignment: Right

11 Click the Type tool to select the text object.

12 Use the arrow keys to align the text.

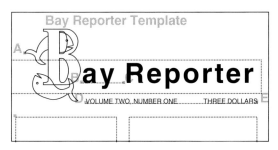

13 Choose the Selection tool; hold down the Shift key and click the baseline of *VOLUME TWO, NUMBER ONE* so that both text objects are selected.

14 Set the paint attributes as follows:

Fill: Black 100

Creating the rectangle

1 Select the Rectangle tool.

2 Scroll left to point F.

3 Drag down diagonally to the bottom-right edge of the guide box.

4 Set the paint attributes as follows:

Fill: Process Color, C-100, M-90, Y-60, K-0
Stroke: None

5 Choose Send to Back from the Edit menu.

6 Choose Preview Illustration from the View menu.

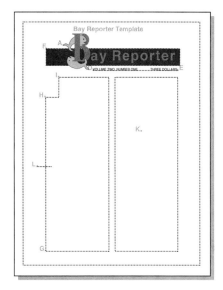

7 Choose Artwork & Template from the View menu.

8 Choose Save from the File menu.

Creating the text block

1 Choose the Zoom-out tool, and click twice in the screen.

2 Select the Type tool.

3 Position the pointer on point G; hold down the mouse button and drag up and right to the other corner of the first guide box.

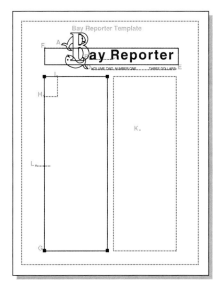

4 Choose the Selection tool.

5 Position the pointer on the anchor point by point G, and hold down the mouse button. Hold down the Shift and Alternate keys and drag right to the second guide box to make a copy of the text object. Release the mouse button and the keys.

6 Hold down the Shift key and click the left text object so that both text objects are selected.

7 Choose Link from the Type menu.

8 Select the Type tool, and click the left text object. You see the blinking insertion point at the top right corner, because the last type you created was right-aligned.

Importing and modifying text

1 Choose Import from the File menu and Text from the submenu, and double-click the file named *WCTXT.SAM*.

2 Choose Select All from the Edit menu.

3 Set the type attributes as follows:

Font: Times-Roman
Size: 10
Leading: 13
Tracking: 0
Alignment: Left

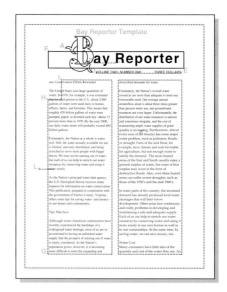

4 Select the Zoom-in tool, and click once near the top of the left text object.

5 Select the Zoom-in tool, and click once toward point H in the template.

6 Select the Type tool.

7 Drag to select the first line of the left text object.

8 Set the type attributes as follows:

Font: Times-Bold
Size: 16
Leading: 18
Tracking: 0

9 Drag to select *Tips That Save* at the bottom of the left column.

10 Set the type attributes as follows:

Font: Times-Bold
Size: 16
Leading: 18
Tracking: 0

11 Choose Actual Size from the View menu.

12 Choose Preview Illustration from the View menu.

13 Choose Artwork & Template from the View menu.

14 Choose Save from the File menu.

Creating a space for the initial cap

Because the large initial capital *W* is outside of the text object, you must first add anchor points and reshape the text object.

1 Using the Type tool, drag to select the *W* in the first headline.

2 Press the Backspace or Delete key to delete the *W*.

3 Select the Zoom-in tool, and click point H.

4 Choose the Add-anchor-point tool, and click the edge of the rectangle near point H and again near point I. This adds anchor points at these two places.

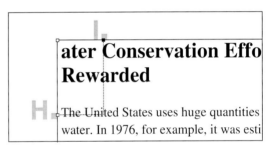

5 Choose the Direct-selection tool.

6 Position the pointer on the top-left corner of the text object, and drag down and right to the guide to make a notch in the text object.

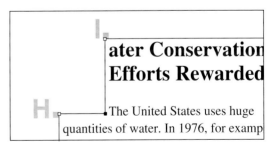

Creating the initial cap

1 Select the Type tool, and click in the white space about an inch to the left of point H.

2 Type a capital **W**.

3 Double-click the *W* to select it.

4 Set the type attributes as follows:

Font: Times-Bold
Size: 85
Horiz. Scale: 60
Auto Leading: On

5 Click the Selection tool. The text object is selected.

6 Choose Create Outlines from the Type menu.

7 Use the arrow keys on the keyboard to move the *W* right and up until the top-right anchor point of the *W* is positioned on the anchor point below point I.

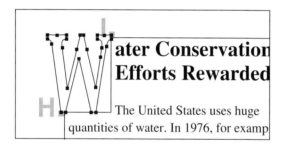

8 Set the paint attributes as follows:

Fill: Process Color, C-100, M-90, Y-60, K-0

9 Choose Preview Illustration from the View menu.

10 Choose Actual Size from the View menu.

11 Choose Artwork & Template from the View menu.

12 Choose Save from the File menu.

Copying the anchor and making the text wrap

1 Choose Open from the File menu, or press Control-O to open an existing file, and double-click the file named *ANCHORART.AI* to open it.

2 Choose Select All from the Edit menu.

3 Choose Copy from the Edit menu.

4 Choose Close from the File menu.

5 Choose Paste from the Edit menu.

6 Choose the Selection tool.

7 Position the pointer on the leftmost tip of the anchor, and drag to point K, near the center of the right text object. (The right edge of the anchor will be off the page.)

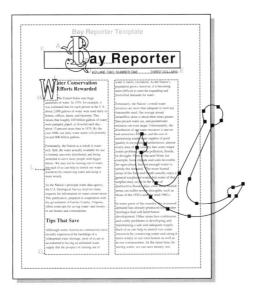

8 Set the paint attributes as follows:

Fill: **Process Color, C-60, M-20, Y-50, K-0**

Making the wrap

1 Hold down the Shift key and click the edge of the right text object so that both the anchor and the text objects are selected.

2 Choose Make Text Wrap from the Type menu.

3 Select the Type tool, position the pointer in the text, and click the mouse button.

4 Choose Select All from the Edit menu.

5 Set the type attributes as follows:

Indentation: Left 3, Right 3

6 Choose the Selection tool, and click away from the artwork to deselect everything.

7 Choose Preview Illustration from the View Menu.

8 Choose Artwork & Template from the View Menu, or press Control-E for the Artwork & Template command.

9 Choose Save from the File menu.

Copying and pasting the graph

1 If necessary, scroll toward the bottom of the page until you can see guide mark L.

2 Choose the Direct-selection tool, and click away from the artwork to deselect everything.

3 Position the pointer on the bottom line of the left text rectangle; hold down the Shift key and drag up to guide mark L.

4 Choose Open from the File menu, and double-click the file named *GRAPHART.AI*.

5 Choose Select All from the Edit menu, or press Control-A for the Select All command.

6 Choose Copy from the Edit menu.

7 Choose Close from the File menu.

8 Choose Paste from the Edit menu.

9 Choose the Selection tool, and drag the graph until the top line is on the bottom of the left text rectangle.

Adding a line and a footer

1 Select the Pen tool.

2 Position the pointer on point G, and click the mouse button.

3 Hold down the Shift key, move the pointer to the right side of the right column, and click to draw a line beneath both columns.

4 Set the paint attributes as follows:

Fill: None
Stroke: Process Color, C-100, M-90, Y-60, K-0
Weight: 2

5 Select the Type tool.

6 Position the pointer just below the line you just drew, in the center of the column, and click the mouse button.

7 Type **July / August**.

8 Choose Select All from the Edit menu.

9 Set the type attributes as follows:

Font: Helvetica
Size: 10
Tracking: 0
Alignment: Centered

10 Choose the Selection tool, and click away from the artwork to deselect everything.

11 Choose Preview Illustration from the View menu.

12 Choose Save from the File menu.

13 Choose Print from the File menu.

14 Choose Close from the File menu.

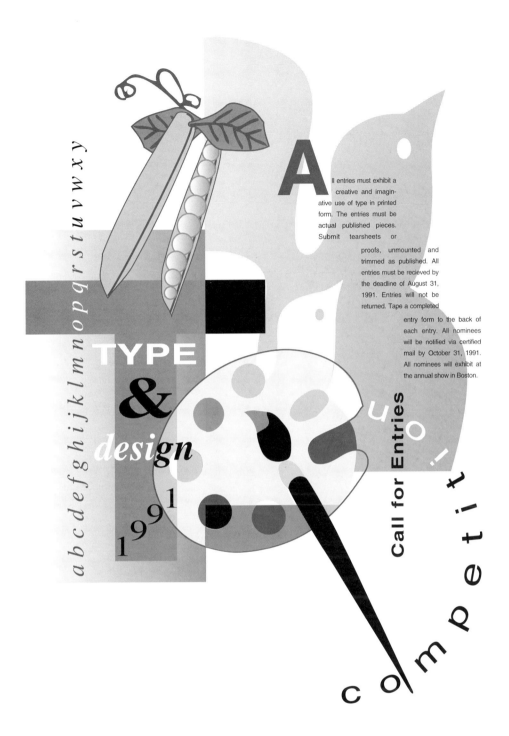

abcdefghijklmnopqrstuvwxy

TYPE
&
design
1991

All entries must exhibit a creative and imaginative use of type in printed form. The entries must be actual published pieces. Submit tearsheets or proofs, unmounted and trimmed as published. All entries must be recieved by the deadline of August 31, 1991. Entries will not be returned. Tape a completed entry form to the back of each entry. All nominees will be notified via certified mail by October 31, 1991. All nominees will exhibit at the annual show in Boston.

Call for Entries

competition!

Lesson

13

LESSON 13: SEED PACKAGE DESIGN

This lesson is a directed study project designed to give you an opportunity to practice what you have learned in lessons 7–10, and earlier. The goal of special projects is to give you the time to apply the tools and techniques you have learned.

In this lesson, you will create these seed packages.

SEED PACKAGE 1

You begin by creating the background rectangles for all four of the seed packages. Depending on the amount of time you have, you may mant to create one seed package or all four.

Opening the files

1 Choose Open from the File menu, or press Control-O to open an existing file. Double-click the file named *SPGUIDE.AI* to open the file.

2 Choose Preferences from the Edit menu, and click Picas/Points under Ruler Units. Notice that there are four rectangular areas numbered 1 through 4. Each area represents one seed package.

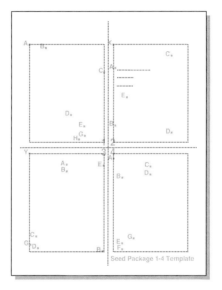

Seed Package 1-4 Template

Creating the background rectangles

1 Scroll until seed package 1, the top-left rectangle, is in the center of the screen.

2 Select the Rectangle tool, and click point A of seed package 1.

3 Type **234** for Width, type **294** for Height, and click OK.

TIP: PRESS CONTROL-
ALT-SPACEBAR TO
ZOOM OUT.

4 Choose the Selection tool.

5 Position the pointer on the top-left anchor point of the rectangle, and drag right to guide corner X, holding down both the Alternate and Shift keys. You now have two rectangles.

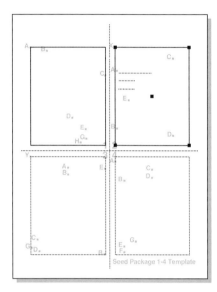

6 Hold down the Shift key and click the left rectangle so that both rectangles are selected.

7 Position the pointer on the top-left anchor point of the left rectangle, and drag down to corner guide Y, holding down both the Alternate and Shift keys. You now have four rectangles, one for each seed package.

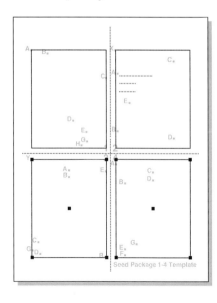

Painting the background rectangle

1 Click the edge of the top-left rectangle to select it.

2 Set the paint attributes as follows:

Fill: Process Color, C-0, M-10, Y-70, K-0
Stroke: Black
Weight: 1

3 Choose Save As from the File menu.

4 Type **SPART1.AI**, and click Save.

Creating the small vines

1 Choose Open from the File menu, and double-click the file named *PGUIDE.AI*.

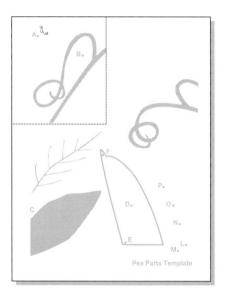

2 Choose the Selection tool.

3 Click to select the small vines near point A. Notice that the vines are grouped.

4 Select the Reflect-dialog tool.

5 Click the top anchor point of the selected vines.

6 Click Vertical Axis, and click Copy.

7 Choose Move from the Edit menu.

8 Type **-27** for Vertical, and click OK.

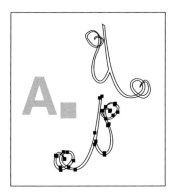

9 Choose the Selection tool.

10 Hold down the Shift key and click the original vine so that both vines are selected.

11 Choose Group from the Arrange menu, or press Control-G for the Group command.

12 Choose Copy from the Edit menu.

13 Choose *SPART.AI* from the Window menu.

14 Select the Zoom-in tool, and click point B in the upper-left rectangle.

15 Choose Paste from the Edit menu, or press Control-V for the Paste command.

Transforming the vine

1 Choose the Selection tool.

2 Position the pointer on the topmost anchor point of the vines, and drag to point B.

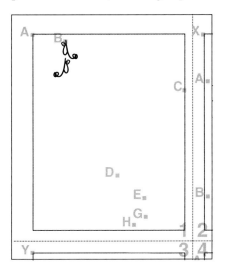

3 Choose Move from the Edit menu.

4 Type **0** for Horizontal, type **-53** for Vertical, and click Copy.

5 Choose Transform Again from the Arrange menu, or press Control-D three times.

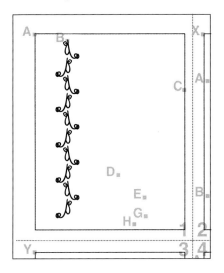

6 Hold down the Shift key and click each vine to select all of the vines.

7 Choose Group from the Arrange menu.

8 Set the paint attributes as follows:

Fill: **Process Color, C-90, M-0, Y-100, K-50**

9 Choose Save from the File menu.

Creating the large vine

1 Choose *PGUIDE.AI* from the Window menu.

2 Select the Auto Trace tool, and click the outside of the large vine (labeled B).

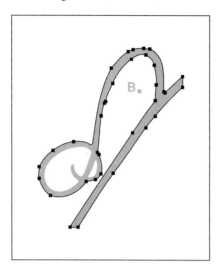

3 Click to autotrace the two inner areas in the bottom-left part of the large vine.

4 Choose the Selection tool.

5 Hold down the Shift key, and click to select all three parts of the vine.

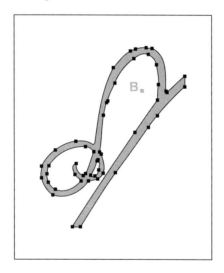

6 Set the paint attributes as follows:

**Fill: Process Color, C-75, M-0, Y-100, K-0
Stroke: None**

7 Choose Make Compound from the Paint menu.

8 Choose Copy from the Edit menu, or press Control-Ins for the Copy command.

9 Choose *SPART.AI* from the Window menu.

10 Choose Paste from the Edit menu, or press Shift-Ins for the Paste command.

Adjusting the location of the vine

1 Choose the Selection tool.

2 Drag the vine so that it is positioned inside the rectangle, with the bottom of the vine just inside the bottom of the rectangle.

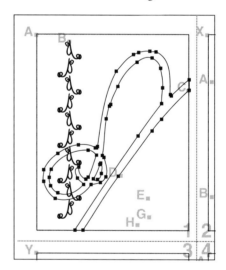

3 Select the small vines.

4 Choose Bring To Front from the Edit menu.

5 Click away from the artwork to deselect everything.

6 Choose Preview Illustration from the View menu, or press Control-Y for the Preview command.

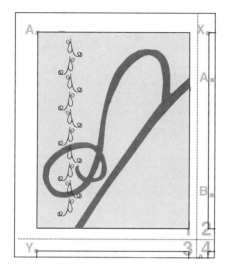

7 Choose Artwork & Template from the Edit menu.

8 Choose Save from the File menu.

Creating text on the seed package

1 Select the Type tool.

2 Click point D, and type **Peas**.

3 Double-click *Peas* to select the entire word.

4 Set the Type attributes as follows:

Font: Times-Italic
Size: 33.5
Tracking: 100
Horiz. Scale: 100
Auto Leading: On

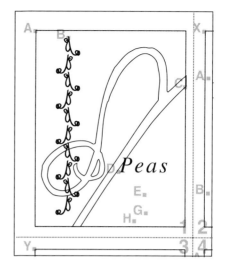

5 Drag to select the *P* in *Peas*.

6 Set the font size to 84.

7 Position the pointer between the *P* and the *e*, and click the mouse button to set an insertion point.

8 Hold down the Alternate key and press the Left Arrow key on the keyboard to kern the letters closer together.

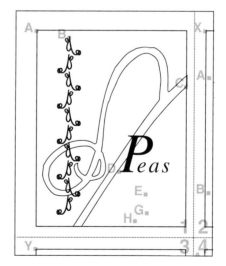

9 Click the Type tool in the toolbox.

10 Click point E. (Before you click, make sure that the pointer is an I-beam inside a dotted box.)

11 Set the type attributes as follows:

Font: Times-Roman
Size: 16.75
Leading: 18.5
Kerning: 0
Tracking: 100
Horiz. Scale: 100
Alignment: Centered

Adding additional type

1 Type **Penelope's**, and press Return.

2 Type **Fresh Seeds**.

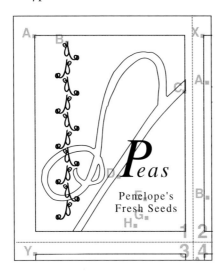

3 Click the Type tool in the toolbox.

4 Click point G. (Before you click, make sure that the pointer is an I-beam inside a dotted box.)

5 Type **Net Weight 17g.** (Include the period.)

6 Choose Select All from the Edit menu.

7 Set the type attributes as follows:

Font: Helvetica
Size: 8.5
Tracking: 100
Horiz. Scale: 100
Auto Leading: On
Alignment: Centered

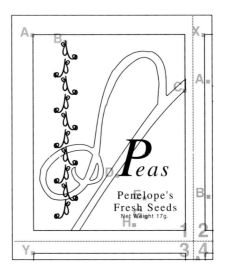

8 Click the Type tool in toolbox.

9 Click point H.

Importing additional type

1 Choose Import from the File menu and Text from the submenu. Double-click the file named *CITIES.TXT*.

2 Choose Select All from the Edit menu.

3 Set the type attributes as follows:

Font: Times-Bold
Size: 5
Tracking: 0
Horiz. Scale: 100
Auto Leading: On
Alignment: Centered

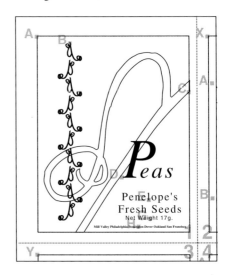

4 Choose the Selection tool.

5 If necessary, use the arrow keys to position the text inside the rectangle.

6 Hold down the Shift key and click the baselines to select all four text objects.

7 Set the paint attributes as follows:

Fill: **Process Color, C-90, M-0, Y-100, K-50**

8 Click away from the artwork to deselect everything.

9 Choose Actual size from the View menu, or press Control-H for the Actual Size command.

10 Choose Preview Illustration from the View menu.

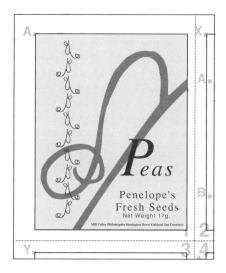

11 Choose Artwork & Template from the View menu.

12 Choose Save from the File menu.

13 Choose Print from the File menu.

SEED PACKAGE 2

In this part of the lesson you will create this seed package.

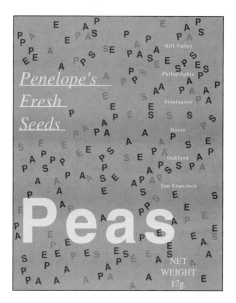

Opening the files

Which files you open depends upon whether or not you have completed seed package 1.

• If you have just completed seed package 1, skip to "Painting the Background Rectangle" below.

• If you have completed seed package 1 and have closed the files, choose Open from the File menu to open *SPART1.AI* and place *SP14TMP.TIF*.

• If you have not completed seed package 1, you must go back to the beginning of that section and complete "Opening the Files" and "Creating the background rectangles" before you go on to step 1 below.

Painting the background rectangle

1 Check to make sure that you have chosen Picas/Points under Ruler Units in the Preferences dialog box.

2 Scroll until seed package 2, the top-right rectangle, is in the center of the screen.

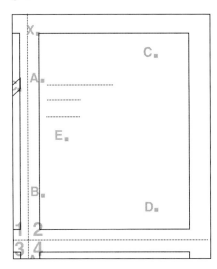

3 Choose the Selection tool.

4 Click the rectangle to select it.

5 Set the paint attributes as follows:

Fill: Process Color, C-50, M-0, Y-100, K-0
Stroke: Black
Weight: 1

6 Choose Lock from the Arrange menu.

Creating text

1 Click away from the artwork to deselect everything.

2 Select the Type tool.

3 Click point A on seed package 2. (Before you click, make sure that the pointer is an I-beam in a dotted box.)

4 Type **Penelope's**, and press Return.

5 Type **Fresh**, and press Return.

6 Type **Seeds**.

7 Drag to select all three lines.

8 Set the type attributes as follows:

Font: Times-Italic
Size: 20
Auto Leading: On
Horiz. Scale: 100
Alignment: Left

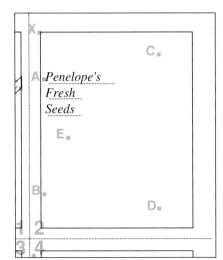

9 Click the Type tool in the toolbox.

10 Choose Save As from the File menu.

11 Type **SPART2.AI**, and click Save.

Drawing the lines

1 Choose the Zoom-in tool, and click point A.

2 Select the Pen tool.

3 Click the left end of the guide under *Penelope's*.

4 Hold down the Shift key and click the right end of the guide.

5 Click the Pen tool in the toolbox.

6 Use the Pen tool to create the lines under *Fresh* and under *Seeds*.

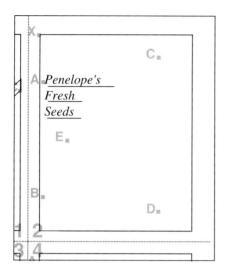

7 Choose the Selection tool.

8 Hold down the Shift key and click to select all three lines.

9 Set the paint attributes as follows:

Fill: None
Stroke: Process Color, C-0, M-10, Y-70, K-0

Creating the "Peas" text on the seed package

1 Select the Type tool.

2 Click point B, and type **Peas**.

3 Double-click the word.

4 Set the type attributes as follows:

Font: Helvetica-Bold
Size: 67
Tracking: 100
Auto Leading: On
Horiz. Scale: 100

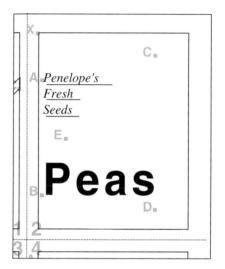

5 Choose Actual Size from the View menu.

Importing text for the seed package

1 Click the Type tool in the toolbox.

2 Click point C toward the top-right corner.

3 Choose Import from the File menu and Text from the submenu.

4 Double-click the file named *CITIES.TXT*. The text is large because of the last font size you set.

5 Choose Select All from the Edit menu.

6 Set the type attributes as follows:

Font: Times-Bold
Size: 5.5
Leading: 30
Tracking: 100
Horiz. Scale: 100
Alignment: Centered

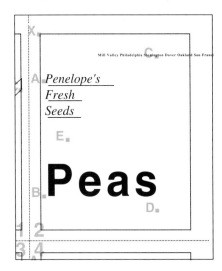

7 Select the Zoom-in tool, and click once near the beginning of the Cities list.

8 Click the Type tool in the toolbox.

9 Position the pointer at the end of each city name, click the mouse button, and press Return.

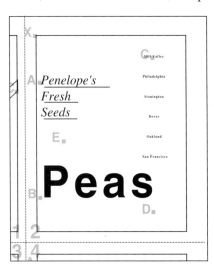

10 Click the Type tool in the toolbox.

Adding the "NET WEIGHT" text

1 Click point D below the *s* in *Peas*.

2 Type (in all capital letters) **NET**, and press Return.

3 Type **WEIGHT**, and press Return.

4 Type **17g.** (Include the period.)

5 Drag to select all three lines of type.

6 Set the type attributes as follows:

Font: Times-Roman
Size: 10
Tracking: 0
Horiz. Scale: 100
Auto Leading: On
Alignment: Centered

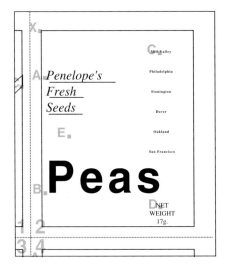

Setting paint attributes to the text

1 Scroll so that the entire package fits on the screen.

2 Choose the Selection tool. Click away from the artwork to deselect everything.

3 Hold down the Shift key and click the baselines to select the text at point A and point B.

4 Set the paint attributes as follows:

Fill: Process Color, C-0, M-10, Y-70, K-0

5 Click away from the artwork to deselect everything.

6 Hold down the Shift key and click to select the text at point C and point D.

7 Set the paint attributes as follows:

Fill: Process Color, C-90, M-0, Y-100, K-50

Creating the random letters on the seed package

1 Select the Type tool.

2 Click point E, and type **P**.

3 Double-click to select the text.

4 Set the type attributes as follows:

Font: Helvetica-Bold
Size: 10
Horiz. Scale: 100

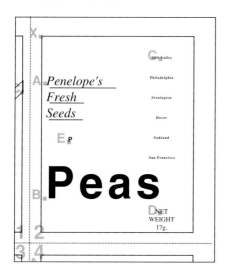

5 Click the Type tool in the toolbox.

6 Click elsewhere on the screen, and type **E**.

7 Repeat steps 5 and 6 for the *A* and the *S*.

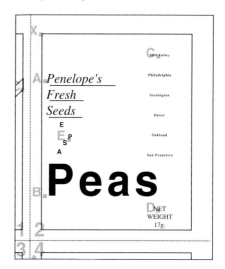

Copying and placing the letters on the package

1 Choose the Selection tool.

2 Hold down the Shift key and click to select all four letters.

3 Use the Alternate key to copy the letters around the seed package.

4 Click away from the artwork to deselect everything.

5 Hold down the Shift key and click to select different letters.

6 Select the Rotate tool.

7 Rotate and copy letters at different angles.

8 Hold down the Shift key and click to select letters randomly.

9 Set the paint attributes as follows:

   Fill: Process Color, C-75, M-0, Y-100, K-0

10 Move any letters that overlap each other.

11 Choose Preview Illustration from the View menu.

12 Choose Artwork & Template from the View menu.

13 Choose Save from the File menu.

14 Choose Print from the File menu.

SEED PACKAGE 3

In this part of the lesson, you will create this seed package.

Opening the files

Which files you open depends upon whether or not you have completed seed package 1.

• If you have just completed seed package 2, skip to "Painting the Background Rectangle" below.

• If you have completed seed package 1 or seed package 2 and have closed the files, open *SPART1.AI* or *SPART2.AI*, along with *SPART14TMP.AI*, by using the Alternate-Open command.

• If you have not completed seed package 1, you must go back to the beginning of that section and complete "Opening the Files" and "Creating the background rectangles" before you go on to step 1.

Painting the background rectangle

1 Check to make sure that you have chosen Picas/Points under Ruler Units in the Preferences dialog box.

2 Scroll until seed package 3, the lower-left rectangle, is in the center of the screen.

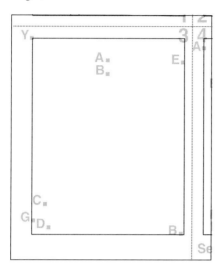

3 Choose the Selection tool.

4 Click the rectangle to select it.

5 Set the paint attributes as follows:

Fill: None
Stroke: Black
Weight: 1

6 Choose Lock from the Arrange menu.

Creating the text on the seed package

1 Select the Type tool.

2 Click point A, and type **PEAS**.

3 Double-click the text to select it.

4 Set the type attributes as follows:

Font: Times-Bold
Size: 25
Tracking: -60
Horiz. Scale: 100
Auto Leading: On
Alignment: Centered

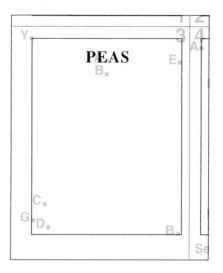

5 Click the Type tool in the toolbox.

6 Click point B, and type **Penelope's Fresh Seeds**.

7 Drag to select the text.

8 Set the type attributes as follows:

Font: Times-Bold
Size: 15.5
Tracking: 0
Auto Leading: On
Alignment: Centered

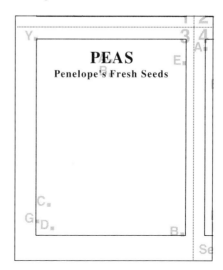

9 Choose Save As from the File menu.

10 Type **SPART3.AI**, and click Save.

Importing text for the seed package

1 Click the Type tool in the toolbox.

2 Click point C.

3 Choose Import from the File menu and Text from the submenu, and double-click the file named *CITIES.TXT.*

4 Choose Select All from the Edit menu.

5 Set the type attributes as follows:

Font: Times-Bold
Size: 8
Leading: 12
Tracking: 0
Alignment: Left

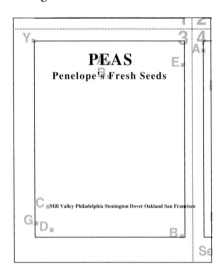

6 Select the Zoom-in tool, and click once on the text.

7 Select the Type tool.

8 Click after *Philadelphia*, and press Enter.

9 Click after *Dover*, and press Enter.

10 Drag to select the space between *Mill Valley* and *Philadelphia*. Type a *space*, a *slash* (/), and a *space*. Make sure that there is a space on each side of the slash. Repeat the process for the other cities.

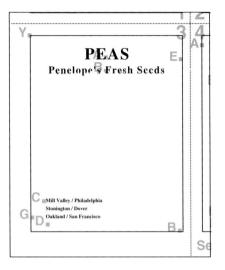

11 Click the Type tool in the toolbox.

12 Click point D, and type **NET WEIGHT 17g.** (Include the period.)

13 Drag to select the text.

14 Set the type attributes as follows:

Font: Times-Roman
Size: 8.8
Tracking: 0

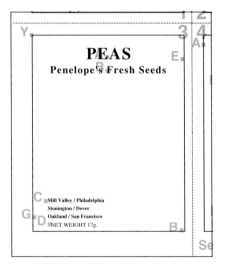

Setting paint attributes to the text

1 Choose Actual Size from the View menu.

2 Scroll to position seed package 3 in the center of the screen.

3 Choose the Selection tool.

4 Hold down the Shift key and click to select the text at points A, B, C, and D.

5 Set the paint attributes as follows:

Fill: Process Color, C-90, M-0, Y-100, K-50

6 Click away from the artwork to deselect everything.

7 Choose Preview Illustration from the View menu.

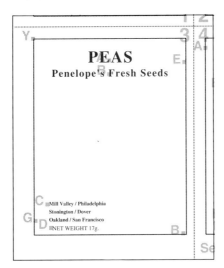

8 Choose Artwork & Template from the View menu.

Drawing the leaf

1 Choose *PGUIDE.AI* from the Window menu, if the file is already open.

2 Select the Auto Trace tool, and click the edge of the leaf surrounding point C.

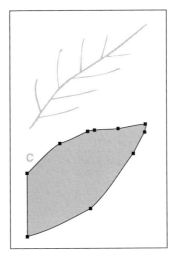

3 Set the paint attributes as follows:

Fill: Process Color, C-75, M-0, Y-100, K-0
Stroke: Process Color, C-90, M-0, Y-100, K-50
Weight: 1

4 Autotrace the leaf veins above the leaf.

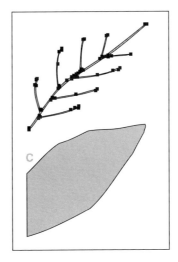

5 Set the paint attributes as follows:

Fill: Process Color, C-90, M-0, Y-100, K-50
Stroke: None

6 Choose the Object-selection tool.

7 Click away from the artwork to deselect it.

8 Drag the vein down onto the leaf.

9 Hold down the Shift key and click the leaf so that the veins and the leaf are selected.

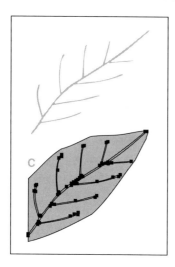

10 Choose Group from the Arrange menu.

Drawing the pea pod

1 Select the Auto Trace tool, and autotrace the pea pod labeled D.

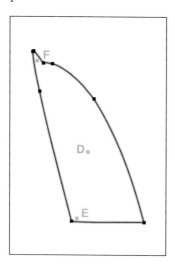

2 Set the paint attributes as follows:

Fill: Process Color, C-75, M-0, Y-100, K-0
Stroke: Process Color, C-90, M-0, Y-100, K-50
Weight: 1

3 Select the Pen tool.

4 Click point E.

5 Move the pointer up to point F, and click to draw the line on the pea pod.

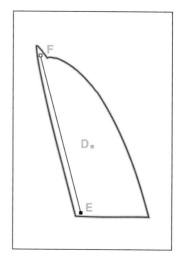

6 Set the paint attributes as follows:

Fill: None
Stroke: Process Color, C-90, M-0, Y-100, K-50
Weight: 2

7 Choose the Object-selection tool.

8 Hold down the Shift key and click to select both the pea pod and the line.

9 Choose Group from the Arrange menu.

Drawing the peas

1 Select the Centered-oval tool.

2 Click point L, type **93** for Width, type **93** for Height, and click OK.

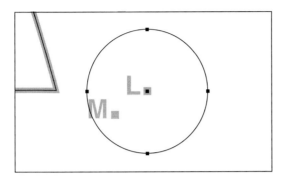

3 Set the paint attributes as follows:

Fill: Process Color, C-50, M-0, Y-100, K-0
Stroke: None

4 Using the Centered-oval tool, click point M.

5 Type **29** for Width, type **17** for Height, and click OK.

6 Select the Rotate-dialog tool.

7 Click point M, type **-45** for Angle, and click OK.

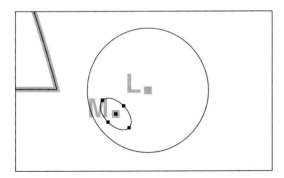

8 Set the paint attributes as follows:

Fill: Process Color, C-0, M-10, Y-70, K-0
Stroke: None

9 Choose the Selection tool.

10 Hold down the Shift key and click to select both ovals.

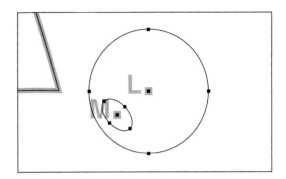

11 Choose Group from the Arrange menu.

Blending the peas

1 Select the Blend tool.

2 Click the bottom leftmost anchor point on the small oval.

3 Click the leftmost anchor point on the large oval.

4 Type **12** for Steps, and click OK.

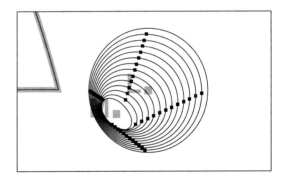

5 Choose the Selection tool.

6 Drag a selection marquee around the entire blend.

7 Choose Group from the Arrange menu.

Copying and scaling the blended peas

1 Position the pointer on the anchor point at point L, and drag to point N, holding down the Alternate key to make a copy.

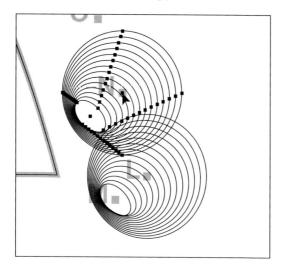

2 Position the pointer on the anchor point at point N, and drag to point O, holding down the Alternate key to make a copy.

3 Position the pointer on the anchor point at point O, and drag to point P, holding down the Alternate key to make a copy.

4 Select the blended oval at point N.

5 Select the Scale-dialog tool.

6 Click point N, type **95** for Uniform Scale, and click OK.

7 Choose the Selection tool.

8 Select the blended oval at point O.

9 Select the Scale-dialog tool.

10 Click point O, type **75** for Uniform Scale, and click OK.

11 Choose the Selection tool or hold down the Control key to access the Selection tool.

12 Select the blended oval at point P.

13 Select the Scale-dialog tool.

14 Click point P, type **55** for Uniform Scale, and click OK.

Adjusting the layering order of the peas

1 Choose the Selection tool.

2 Click oval L.

3 Choose Send To Back from the Edit menu.

4 Click oval N, and choose Send To Back from the Edit menu.

5 Click oval O, and choose Send To Back from the Edit menu.

6 Click oval P, and choose Send To Back from the Edit menu.

7 Hold down the Shift key and click to select all the peas.

8 Choose Group from the Arrange menu.

9 Drag the peas onto the pea pod labeled D.

10 Choose Bring to Front from the Edit menu.

11 Hold down the Shift key and click the pea pod so that both the pea pod and the peas are selected.

12 Choose Group from the Arrange menu.

Drawing the vine

1 Choose Preferences from the Edit menu, or press Control-K for the Preferences command, type **1** for Freehand Tolerance, and click OK.

2 Select the Auto Trace tool, and autotrace the outside of the vine that is above and to the right of the pea pod.

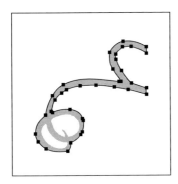

3 Autotrace the two inside areas of the vine.

4 Choose the Object-selection tool.

5 Hold down the Shift key and click all three pieces of the vine to select them.

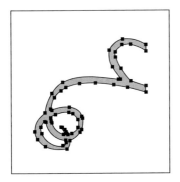

6 Set the paint attributes as follows:

Fill: **Process Color, C-90, M-0, Y-100, K-50**

7 Choose Make Compound from the Paint menu.

Copying the artwork for the seed package

1 Hold down the Shift key and click to select the leaf, pea pod, and vine.

2 Choose Copy from the Edit menu.

3 Choose *SPART3.AI* from the Window menu.

4 Choose Paste from the Edit menu.

5 Choose the Zoom-out tool, and click once.

6 Choose the Selection tool.

7 Click away from the artwork to deselect everything.

Assembling the artwork on the seed package

1 Position the pointer on the bottom anchor point of the leaf, and drag to point G.

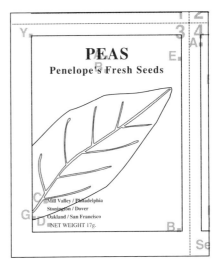

2 Position the pointer on the bottom-right anchor point of the pea pod, and drag to point F.

3 Position the pointer on the top-right anchor point of the vine, and drag to point E.

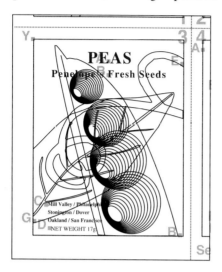

4 Choose the Selection tool.

5 Hold down the Shift key and click to select all of the type objects.

6 Choose Bring To Front from the Edit menu.

Modifying the paint attributes of the text

1 Select the Type tool.

2 Drag to select the first *S* in *Seeds*.

3 Set the paint attributes as follows:

Fill: White
Stroke: None

4 Choose the Selection tool, and click away from the artwork to deselect everything.

5 Choose Preview Illustration from the View menu.

Note: To save time, you can drag a selection marquee around a seed package and choose Preview Selection from the View menu to see a preview of only the selection.

6 Choose Artwork & Template from the View menu.

7 Choose Save from the File menu.

8 Choose Print from the File menu.

9 Close the file named *PGUIDE.AI*. Do not save changes.

SEED PACKAGE 4

In this part of the lesson, you will create this seed package.

Opening the files

Which files you open depends upon whether or not you have completed another seed package.

• If you have just completed any other seed package, skip to "Painting the background rectangle" below.

• If you have completed another seed package and have closed the files, choose Open from the File menu to open *SPART1.AI*, *SPART2.AI*, or *SPART3.AI* and *SP14TMP.TIF*.

• If you have not completed seed package 1, you must go back to the beginning of that section and complete "Opening the files" and "Creating the background rectangles" before you go on to step 1 below.

Painting the background rectangle

1 Check to make sure that you have chosen Picas/Points under Ruler Units in the Preferences dialog box.

2 Scroll until seed package 4, the bottom-right rectangle, is in the center of the screen.

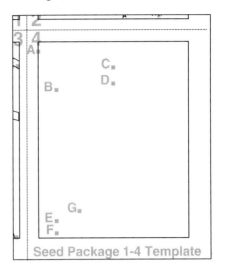

3 Choose the Selection tool.

4 Click the rectangle to select it.

5 Set the paint attributes as follows:

Fill: None
Stroke: Black
Weight: 1

6 Choose Lock from the Arrange menu.

7 Select the Rectangle tool.

8 Click point A, type **234** for Width, type **30** for Height, and click OK.

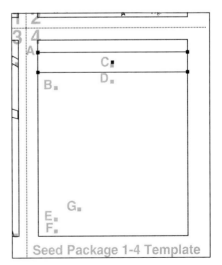

9 If necessary, use the arrow keys on the keyboard to line up the rectangle with the background rectangle.

10 Set the paint attributes as follows:

Fill: Process Color, C-90, M-0, Y-100, K-50
Stroke: None

11 Using the Rectangle tool, click point B.

12 Type **175** for Width, type **185** for Height, and click OK.

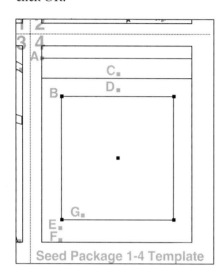

13 Set the paint attributes as follows:

Fill: Process Color, C-0, M-10, Y-70, K-0
Stroke: Black
Weight: 1

14 Choose Preview Illustration from the View menu.

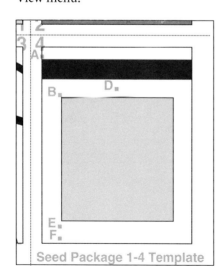

15 Choose Artwork & Template from the View menu.

16 Choose Save As from the File menu.

17 Type **SPART4.AI**, and click Save.

Creating "Peas" text on the seed package

1 Select the Type tool, click point C, and type **PEAS**.

2 Double-click the type to select it.

3 Set the type attributes as follows:

Font: Helvetica-Bold
Size: 24
Tracking: 100
Horiz. Scale: 100
Alignment: Centered

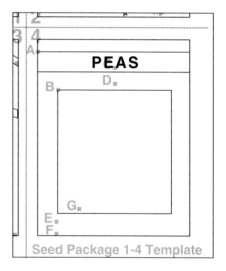

4 Set the paint attributes as follows:

Fill: White

Adding more text on the seed package

1 Click the Type tool in the toolbox.

2 Click point D, and type **Penelope's Fresh Seeds**.

3 Drag to select the text.

4 Set the type attributes as follows:

Font: Times-Roman
Size: 15.32
Tracking: 100
Horiz. Scale: 100

Adding "NET WEIGHT" text to the seed package

1 Click the Type tool in the toolbox.

2 Click point E, and type **NET WEIGHT 17g.** (Include the period.)

3 Drag to select the text.

4 Set the type attributes as follows:

Font: Times-Roman
Size: 10
Tracking: 100
Horiz. Scale: 100
Alignment: Left

Importing text to the seed package

1 Click the Type tool in the toolbox.

2 Click point F.

3 Choose Import from the File menu and Text from the submenu, and double-click the file named *CITIES.TXT*.

4 Choose Select All from the Edit menu.

5 Set the type attributes as follows:

Font: Times-Bold
Size: 5
Tracking: 106
Horiz. Scale: 100
Alignment: Left

6 Choose the Selection tool; then hold down the Shift key and click to select the text at points D, E, and F.

7 Set the paint attributes as follows:

Fill: Black

8 Choose Save from the File menu.

Creating the pea pods

1 Choose New from the File menu.

2 Choose Place Template from the File menu, and double-click the file named *SP4TMP.TIF*.

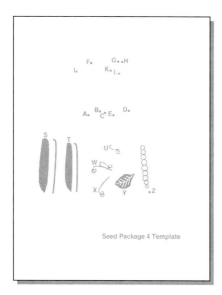

3 Select the Auto Trace tool.

4 Autotrace pea pod S.

5 Autotrace pea pod T.

6 Choose the Selection tool.

7 Hold down the Shift key and click to select both pea pods.

8 Set the paint attributes as follows:

Fill: Process Color, C-75, M-0, Y-100, K-0
Stroke: Process Color, C-90, M-0, Y-100, K-50
Weight: .72

Creating detail on the pea pod using the pen tool

1 Select the Pen tool.

2 Draw the line next to pea pod S.

3 Choose the Object-selection tool, and click to select the entire line.

4 Choose Group from the Arrange menu.

5 Select the Pen tool, and draw the line next to pea pod T.

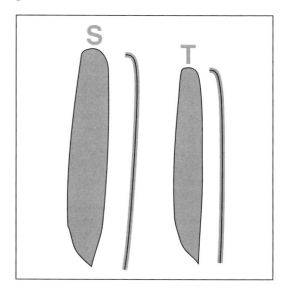

6 Choose the Object-selection tool, and click to select the entire line.

7 Choose Group from the Arrange menu.

8 Choose the Selection tool.

9 Hold down the Shift key and click to select both lines.

10 Set the paint attributes as follows:

Fill: None
Stroke: Process Color, C-90, M-0, Y-100, K-50
Weight: 1.5

11 Click away from the artwork to deselect it.

Moving the pea pod elements

1 Select the line next to pea pod S.

2 Choose Move from the Edit menu.

3 Type **-25** for Horizontal, and click OK.

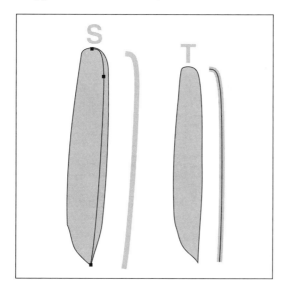

4 Use the Selection tool to select all parts of pea pod S.

5 Choose Group from the Arrange menu.

6 Select the line next to pea pod T.

7 Choose Move from the Edit menu.

8 Type **-18** for Horizontal, and click OK.

9 Select all parts of pea pod T.

10 Choose Group from the Arrange menu.

Creating the vines

1 Select the Zoom-in tool, and click vine W.

2 Select the Auto Trace tool.

3 Autotrace all parts of vines U, W, and X, tracing the outside of the vines before you trace the inside.

4 Choose the Selection tool.

5 Drag a marquee to select all three vines.

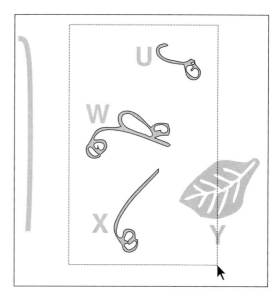

6 Set the paint attributes as follows:

Fill: Process Color, C-90, M-0, Y-100, K-50
Stroke: None

7 Click away from the artwork to deselect everything.

8 Choose Preview Illustration from the View menu.

9 Choose Artwork & Template from the View menu.

10 Drag a marquee to select all parts of vine U.

11 Choose Make Compound from the Paint menu.

12 Repeat the above two steps to select vine W and make it a compound path.

13 Repeat the process again to select vine X and make it a compound path.

14 Choose Preview Illustration from the View menu.

15 Choose Artwork & Template from the View menu.

16 Choose Save from the File menu.

Drawing the leaf

1 Select the Auto Trace tool.

2 Autotrace the outside edge of leaf Y.

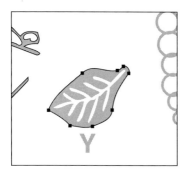

3 Set the paint attributes as follows:

Fill: Process Color, C-75, M-0, Y-100, K-0
Stroke: Process Color, C-90, M-0, Y-100, K-50
Weight: 1

4 Autotrace the veins of the leaf.

5 Set the paint attributes as follows:

Fill: Process Color, C-90, M-0, Y-100, K-50
Stroke: None

6 Choose the Object-selection tool.

7 Select the leaf and the veins.

8 Choose Group from the Arrange menu.

Drawing the peas

1 Choose Actual Size from the View menu.

2 Select the Centered-oval tool.

3 Position the pointer in the center of the top pea.

4 Hold down the Shift key and drag to draw the top pea.

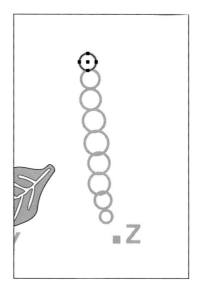

5 Draw all the peas, working from the top to the bottom.

6 Choose the Selection tool.

7 Drag a marquee to select all of the peas.

8 Choose Group from the Arrange menu.

9 Set the paint attributes as follows:

Fill: Process Color, C-50, M-0, Y-100, K-0
Stroke: Process Color, C-100, M-0, Y-100, K-0
Weight: 1

10 Select the Zoom-out tool, and click once.

11 Choose the Selection tool.

12 Position the pointer on the bottom anchor point of pea pod T.

13 Drag to point Z, holding down the Alternate key to make a copy.

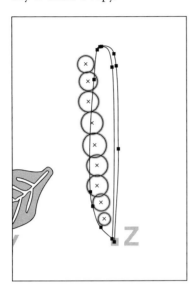

Adjusting the angle of the pea pod using the rotate tool

1 Select the Rotate tool.

2 Click point Z.

3 Hold down the mouse button and drag the top of the pea pod to the left, around the peas.

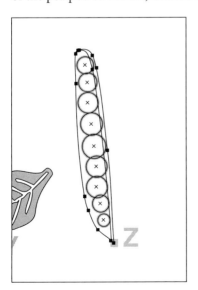

4 Choose Send To Back from the Edit menu.

5 Choose the Selection tool.

6 Drag a marquee to select the peas and the pea pod.

7 Choose Group from the Arrange menu.

8 Choose Save from the File menu.

Assembling the pea pods

1 Position the pointer on the bottom anchor point of the pea pod with the peas, and drag to point C.

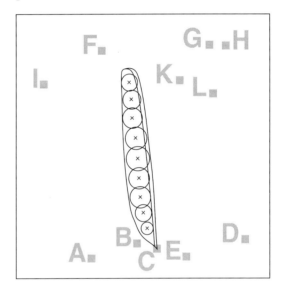

2 Position the pointer on the bottom anchor point of pea pod S, and drag up to point A, holding down the Alternate key to make a copy.

3 Position the pointer on the bottom anchor point of pea pod S, and drag to point B.

4 Select the Rotate-dialog tool.

5 Click point B, type **-21**, and click OK.

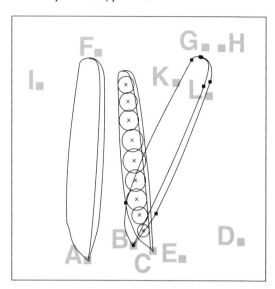

6 Choose the Selection tool.

7 Drag the pea pod from point B to point E, holding down the Alternate key to make a copy.

8 Select the Rotate-dialog tool.

9 Click point E, type **17**, and click OK.

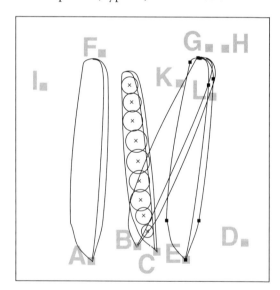

10 Choose the Selection tool.

11 Position the pointer on the bottom anchor point of pea pod T, and drag to point D.

12 Select the Scale-dialog tool.

13 Click point D, type **90** for Uniform Scale, click Preserve Line Weights, and click OK.

14 Selcct the Rotate-dialog tool.

15 Click point D, type **4** for Angle, and click OK.

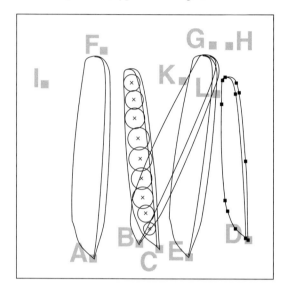

Assembling the vines and leaves

1 Choose the Selection tool.

2 Drag vine U by the top of the stem to point H.

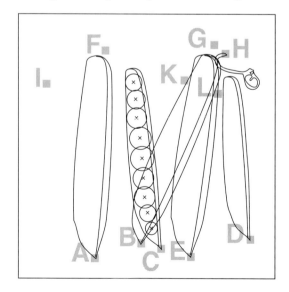

3 Choose Bring To Front from the Edit menu.

4 Position the pointer on the bottom rightmost anchor point of vine W, and drag to point F.

5 Position the pointer on the topmost anchor point of vine X, and drag to point G.

6 Choose Bring To Front from the Edit menu.

7 Position the pointer on the leftmost anchor point of the leaf, and drag to point I.

Adjusting the angle and moving the vines and leaves

1 Choose Move from the Edit menu.

2 Type -**17** for Horizontal, type -**9** for Vertical, and click Copy.

3 Select the Rotate-dialog tool.

4 Click the stem of the new leaf.

5 Type **161.5** for Angle, and click OK.

6 Choose Copy from the Edit menu.

7 Choose Paste In Front from the Edit menu.

8 Choose the Selection tool.

9 Drag the leaf by the stem to point K.

10 Choose the Rotate-dialog tool.

11 Click the stem at point K.

12 Type **42.5** for Angle, and click OK.

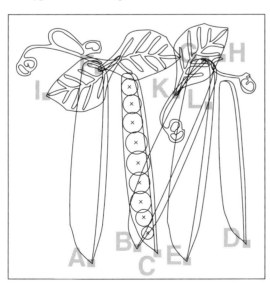

13 Choose the Scale-dialog tool.

14 Click the stem at point K.

15 Click Non-Uniform Scale, type **100** for Horizontal, type **90** for Vertical, and click Copy.

16 Choose the Selection tool.

17 Drag the new leaf by the stem to point L.

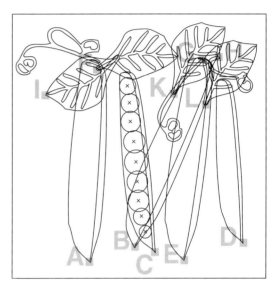

18 Choose Send To Back from the Edit menu.

Grouping and scaling the artwork

1 Click away from the artwork to deselect everything.

2 Choose Preview Illustration from the View menu.

3 Choose Artwork Only from the View menu.

4 Drag a marquee to select all of the artwork (leaves, vines, and pea pods).

5 Choose Group from the Arrange menu.

6 Choose the Scale-dialog tool, and click in the center of the artwork.

7 Click Uniform Scale, type **95**, click Preserve Line Weights, and click OK.

Copying and pasting the artwork

1 Choose Copy from the Edit menu.

2 Choose *SPART4.AI* from the Window menu.

3 Choose Paste from the Edit menu.

4 Choose the Selection tool.

5 Position the pointer on the bottom anchor point of the leftmost pea pod, and drag to point G.

6 Click away from the artwork to deselect everything.

7 Choose Preview Illustration from the View menu.

8 Choose Save from the File menu.

9 Choose Print from the File menu.

10 Close all the files.

COLOPHON

Project and Illustration Designs: Wendy Bell, Dayna Porterfield, Deborah Spark

Writing: Sue Crissman, Lynne Fitzpatrick, Kisa Harris

Illustrations: Jeffrey Schaaf

Book Production: Jeffrey Schaaf

CD Cover Design: Dean Dapkus

Film Production: Cheryl Elder, Karen Winguth

Book Production Management: Kisa Harris

Publication Management: Kisa Harris

Legal advisor: Paul Klein

Special Thanks to: Patrick Ames, Frank Gomaz, Tom Harmon, Carita Klevickis, Glen Pierre, Nora Sandoval

PRODUCTION NOTES

This book was created electronically using FrameMaker on the Macintosh Quadra 800. Art was produced using Adobe Illustrator, Adobe Photoshop, and SnapJot on the Quadra 800. Working film was produced with the PostScript language on an Agfa 5000 Imagesetter. The Minion and Frutiger families of typefaces are used throughout this book.

Adobe Training Resources

The Classroom in a Book™ series of training workbooks guides you through step-by-step lessons to help you learn how to master the many powerful features of Adobe Illustrator.

If finding time to focus is difficult, or if you think an instructor-led training program will augment your learning curve, consider investigating some of the many professional training businesses and educational institutions using this very same Classroom in a Book in their classes. Instructors can provide feedback and guidance that go beyond the contents of this book in a classroom setting.

For suggestions, and the name of a licensed Adobe training resource nearest you: In North America, call **Adobe's Customer Services at 1-800-833-6687.** In Europe and the Pacific Rim, call your local distributor.